Strange Material

STRANGE MATERIAL

STORYTELLING THROUGH TEXTILES

LEANNE PRAIN

Project photography by Jeanie Ow

ARSENAL PULP PRESS · VANCOUVER

ARSENAL PULP PRESS
Suite 202 – 211 East Georgia St.
Vancouver, BC V6A 1Z6
Canada
arsenalpulp.com

The publisher gratefully acknowledges the support of the Canada Council for the Arts and the British Columbia Arts Council for its publishing program, and the Government of Canada (through the Canada Book Fund) and the Government of British Columbia (through the Book Publishing Tax Credit Program) for its publishing activities.

The poem "Day," page 74, copyright © Laura Farina.

Cover photograph: Rosalind Wyatt
Author photograph: Nicol Lischka
Project photography: Jeanie Ow
Photographs on pp. 27, 51, 63, 160, 218 (top): Gerilee McBride
Photographs on pp. 88, 218 (bottom): Leanne Prain

Design by Gerilee McBride
Edited by Susan Safyan

Printed and bound in the Republic of Korea

Library and Archives Canada Cataloguing in Publication:
Prain, Leanne, 1976–, author
    Strange material : storytelling through textiles / Leanne Prain ; project photography by Jeanie Ow.

Includes index.
Issued in print and electronic formats.
ISBN 978-1-55152-550-1 (pbk.).—ISBN 978-1-55152-551-8 (epub)

    1. Textile crafts—Social aspects. 2. Storytelling in art. I. Ow, Jeanie, photographer II. Title.

TT699.P73 2014   746   C2014-904299-X
                                     C2014-904300-7

This book is dedicated to Connie and Dan Prain, my parents, who introduced me to the lifelong pursuit of making things by hand.

You both inspire me every day.

Contents

Introduction

My intention for *Strange Material* is simple. I want you to identify your own stories, and encourage you to share them through handmade work. If you are not motivated to make something with your hands, I hope that the tales shared by the artists within these pages inspire you to look for stories in unlikely pockets of your life. Narrative is the binding thread of human experience, and stories are the medium that we use to know one another and ourselves.

This book was prompted by a series of epiphanies that I experienced while researching my previous book, *Hoopla: The Art of Unexpected Embroidery*. Through the course of interviewing twenty-three artists, I discovered that every conversation was lit with elements of story. Artist Sherri Lynn Wood told me that there was no written history of women's contributions to the world of tattoo arts in the 1990s, yet she captured this historical microcosm through her embroidered Tattoo Baby Doll Project. Aubrey Longley-Cook's stitched animation of his roommate's runaway dog Gus, captured the perpetual motion of Gus's psyche, photographed in two ways:

the satin-stitched front and the gnarled, knotty back. Jenny Hart, well-known in the embroidery world for her illustrative pattern company Sublime Stitching, conceived a fictional band poster that advertised a concert by rock icon Iggy Pop in the hospital room where she had been born. With each exchange, it became apparent to me that rarely are textile works simply end products—they are saturated with narrative, from the chain of events that led to their creation and the choice of materials used, to the stories told by the pieces themselves, and finally to the accounts shared by those who have experienced an emotional reaction to these artworks.

While the commercial crafting mega-stores of the western world promote fashionable tools and materials, there is more substance rooted in most fiber craft than is generally found in trendy appliquéd pillows featuring wildlife or ironically kitschy sweater patterns. Concurrently, the gallery system is widely dismissive of materials associated with "craft" and of artists from artisanal or self-taught backgrounds. It is my desire to illuminate the conversations happening outside

> **Art is communication.**
>
> —*artist Judy Chicago*

these two limited perspectives. Systematically underrepresented in art history, textiles often carry the stories of those whom society overlooks: women, children, slaves, immigrants, Aboriginal peoples, housewives, stay-at-home fathers, the ill, the disappeared, the displaced, and the grieving. We do a disservice to ourselves when we ignore the fact that textiles play an important role in telling our histories. Knitting, weaving, embroidery—no matter what the medium is, textiles are both byproducts and generators of narrative.

I am often asked how I determine which artists should be featured in my books. My response is that my research is willfully imperfect: I choose to write about artists who represent the complexity and diversity of what is happening in contemporary textiles—it is important to me to feature not only artists who work metropolitan areas, but those who create at home and share their work in their local communities or in the hyper-clutter of the online world. Some of the featured artists have spent years studying their craft, and others are self-taught. This shotgun approach is my attempt to initiate multiple conversations about the many ways that textiles are being used right now; to generate dialogue, to chronicle personal histories, to share commonalities, and sometimes, just to delight.

During the course of writing this manuscript, I was approached by a film-industry props master looking for an embroidery artist who could stitch a commissioned work for a film. The request was rather predictable for stitch-work; he was seeking a handkerchief stitched with a medieval landscape, complete with a castle. The movie's princess was supposed to give this piece of embroidery to her prince. Just as mass culture doles out stereotypes around textiles, our early encounters with the idea of story are often similarly limited. As young children, we are told that stories have a hero and villain, a problem and a resulting triumph. But as we

grow into our lives, we discover that most stories are richer and more nuanced. Our tales can sprout from the smallest of items—the grocery list of a departed love one, a receipt kept in a wallet, or a photograph left behind. In school, we are instructed to share our stories by writing from point A to point B, ignoring the fact that we live in a world also steeped in visual and oral storytelling. Textiles are a willing medium for stories both visual and verbal; you can explore poetry through stitching, produce a knitted mask with the face of a strange but familiar character, or work with your community to stitch a quilt on a topical issue.

One of the most effective pieces of advice that I received as an undergraduate student studying creative writing was that a story should have a beginning, a middle, and an end. I hope that this book becomes one small song in a greater chorus of voices exploring how textiles can help us learn about ourselves and those around us. I sense that we are at the beginning of a much larger history and that there are still many stories to be told. The middle and end of this narrative are not apparent yet, and I hope that you will contribute to it by making your own unique work.

Let the artists featured in this book inspire you to take risks with your own artwork. If you are afraid to start, ask yourself, what is the worst that can happen? This is the dare that I offer to you: try something new. Not every project will begin smoothly, but through the process, you can experience the thrill of gaining a new skill or sharing an as-yet unspoken thought. Experimentation always makes for a great story, both on and off the cloth.

....

Howie Woo, *How the Mushroom Fire Started*, 2010, crochet, each mushroom 2 x 2 in (5.08 x 5.08 cm). Photo: Howie Woo. The local news reported that a mushroom farm was destroyed by a massive fire. It was said that bales of hay spontaneously combusted, causing the fire. But this photo—which was captured moments before the blaze—tells the full story.

Chapter One

MAKING MEANING

We are, as a species, addicted to story. Even when the body goes to sleep, the mind stays up all night, telling itself stories.

—**Jonathan Gottschall**, *The Storytelling Animal: How Stories Make Us Human*

Storytelling

Textiles are around us, all of the time. We are intimately connected to cloth: a dress-up costume, a first sewing project, a bed sheet. Textile practices are typically labor intensive, fastidious and repetitive; the intimate nature of such handwork creates a deep connection between the artwork and its maker—and ultimately the viewer. Textiles can be the medium through which I can get closer to you.

—Curator Sarah Quinton, Close to You: Contemporary Textiles, Intimacy and Popular Culture

For as long as there have been human beings, there has been storytelling. Throughout human history, we have communicated in a variety of ways—via paintings left on the walls of caves, in tales told over firelight, through the crash and thunder of a blockbuster movie. It is inherently human to be attracted to narrative; we are the only species that exchanges stories with one another. Whether these tales come through a song, conversational tidbit, handwritten letter, or novel, they allow us to show our commonalities and differences to each other. We can relate to a story or we can learn from it; we can be inspired to change the outcome of a tale, or we can choose to retell it from our own perspective.

For as long as people have been making things by hand, they have been telling stories through their handmade artwork. Tales told in cloth have been collected throughout history. Textile-based stories can be found throughout the world; from the *paj ntaub* story cloths of the Hmong peoples of Laos to the embroidered war narrative of the Norman Conquest and the Battle of Hastings that made up the Bayeux Tapestry to graveyard quilts commemorating the deaths of loved ones made by early American settlers in the 1800s. There, amid the warp and weft, are societal commentary, personal confessions, humor, fictional dalliances, the secret lives of oppressed people, and snapshots of the world as an individual experiences it in his or her lifetime. "Weaving a tale" or "dropping a thread" takes on a new meaning when textiles are viewed as more than functional objects.

Textile-making is often taught through an oral history, with one maker teaching another how to knot, thread, bind, or weave. Storytelling has similar origins: as we learn from each other, we begin to recognize plot, characters, tone, conflict, and resolution—all the elements that make a great story. Just as textiles come in many forms, so do narratives. Throughout these pages, all manner of storytelling will be explored, including memoir, cultural fables, pictorial histories, wearable fictions, political manifestos, narrative retellings, and poetic verse. The artists featured in this book create narratives with a needle instead of a pen, dye rather than ink,

> *Embroidery is a process of conveying and capturing stories.*
> *Behind every embroidered piece there is a story.*
>
> —artist Kirsty Whitlock

cloth in place of paper. This book will encourage you to take your own storytelling off the page and leap into the mediums of stitching, dyeing, fabric painting, embroidery, knitting, crochet, felting, and other fiber arts.

The Safe Space of Textiles

The very materiality of cloth has a sentimental resonance that is not apparent on paper. Some stories are easier to tell through craft.

Many of us remember school for the terror of the marked-up page, bleeding red with the correction of a teacher's pen. Fabric can eliminate the widely experienced phobias surrounding writing and critique. Textiles might be unpicked, but they can't be edited. From bored homemakers to survivors of abuse to leaders of resistance, fabric offers a familiar space on which to share stories that need unraveling. There is no wrong way to tell a story on cloth. The tactile, even comforting, nature of textiles can conjure memories and inspire people to share them.

As author Rosika Parker observed in *The Subversive Stitch*, embroidery has provided both community and solidarity to women throughout history. Sewing circles have allowed women to gather together, swap war stories, and learn from one another. In modern incarnations, they've created a place for all people to discuss issues such as the AIDS crisis through quilts, breast cancer through yarn bombing, and civil disobedience through stitching.

Stitching Overlooked Stories

Textiles are not always taken seriously—in the history of art, there is little recognition of textiles, and the subject is omitted from most critical texts and gallery collections. Textiles are the invisible sister of the art world, and those who make them have to work hard to be seen. Despite this tension, cloth has long been a medium for subversive messages: in the nineteenth century, incarcerated suffragettes passed hankies between each other to share solidarity; in the mid-twentieth century, feminist artist Judy Chicago worked with a team of

I see the sketchbook as really private; you don't share it with anyone,
and you can put whatever you want in it.

—Bettina Matzkuhn

textile artists to chronicle images of childbirth, which was previously widely disregarded in the canon of art history; in the 1970s and '80s, the women of Chile stitched fabrics that told the stories of the "disappeared" generations under the Pinochet dictatorship.

Designing Your Own Narrative Textiles

Both craftspeople and writers are collectors. Writers scrounge for words, phrases, or feelings; crafters pocket bits and bobs, ends of wool, half-spools of thread, a button that might be useful. We store things—a phrase that summarizes an elusive moment, a strange brass clasp that might help bring a garment back to life.

The "Prompts" in this book are meant to encourage you to consider how to bring narrative into your own textile work. Most designers find it helpful to brainstorm their ideas on paper before beginning work in their chosen medium. Use a sketchbook to brainstorm; keep lists, and document stray phrases that come to you. Add to your pages things that inspire you—swatches of fabrics, colors of thread, drawings of buttons, and sketches of your ideas.

When describing the writing process, beat poet Allen Ginsberg once said: "First thought, best thought." The first rule of good writing is to avoid over-thinking. The best writing sounds natural and unforced. Do not try to imitate the style of others. Let whatever you are thinking about fall naturally onto the page, and do not self-censor. Stopping to refine the details will only block your ideas and hamper your creativity. Write what you hear in your head, and use your own unique voice. Editing has no place when generating new ideas—good, bad, ugly, or divine.

Freddie Robins, *Craft Kills*, 2002, machine-knitted wool, knitting needles, 78.74 x 26.77 x 14.96 in (200 x 68 x 38 cm). Photo: Douglas Atfield

Freddie Robins on *Craft Kills*

"When I made Craft Kills, I was thinking about how craft is overlooked, particularly textile crafts and knitting. They are seen as benign, passive activities. Craft is not accepted in the fine art arena. Craft Kills comes from trying to turn this sentiment on its head. What if craft was seen as something dangerous? Something that we aren't allowed to do becomes very, very powerful. Even though there's a big resurgence in knitting, it's still not taken very seriously. I think that makes it a powerful tool, because it's so undervalued and unexpected."

Read a full interview with Freddie Robins on p. 130.

BINDING CLOTHS:
An Interview with Tamar Stone

Artist Tamar Stone creates storybooks out of bed linens and corsets. Having been confined to corsets twice for spinal corrections, her work is inspired by her own experiences of body image and femininity. Her handmade books capture issues of self-esteem and assimilation in the areas of fashion and medical necessity. Tamar has stitched other three-dimensional tales, using bed linens as "pages" in a project that puts women's stories on coverlets, pillowcases, and pillows. In order to read the stories, viewers need to become "intimately involved" with the bed, turning the covers to reveal the whole narrative, and thereby repeating the actions of bed-making, a domestic task that women have been doing for centuries. *tamarstone.com*

Tamar Stone, inside pages of *The Vital System,* "Good Sense," "Little Beauty." Photos: Tamar Stone

Q: How did cloth items, such as corsets and bed sheets, become your canvas for storytelling?

A: I had been working with the idea of women being "bound" by certain conventions, and after making two paper books, I knew I wanted those thoughts to become more three-dimensional so that the stories could be told "out of" the textiles itself. With my first paper book, I had embroidered the title onto the buckle straps that held it together—the same straps that were part of braces that I had worn first for spinal curvature and later, in college, for a herniated disc.

Q: Can you tell me how your bed projects, tiny doll-sized beds, work as a medium to tell a story? Why did you make these linens so that they function as the pages of a book?

A: In order to read these intimate stories the reader must unmake each bed, pulling back the covers to "turn the pages." In order to close the work, one must re-make the bed, mimicking the actions of women's housework as performed over the centuries. I wanted to alternate between intimate stories and things that were told to women by an outside "professional" source, since women have always been given advice by their physicians or in magazines, or to each other. I also wanted to weave stories of relationships through history: the fitted-sheet story is about a girl asking for information on birth control without using specific words, as in the past it was illegal to obtain birth control via the US postal system. Another story on the mattress describes a marriage that wasn't very good, but ultimately resulted in love for one of the widowed partners.

H.T.W.E. ("...*His Thanks Was Enough*...") (p. 22) began with my interest in Florence Nightingale and her hospital reform

This is the end of a long and tedious journey, 2010, antique collapsible wooden doll bed with slatted mattress support, wool and cotton blankets, linens, embroidery thread, 12 x 21 x 14 in (30.48 x 53.34 x 35.56 cm). Photo: Tamar Stone. "These are stories of women who traveled across the country on the Overland Trail during the 1800s. They came from a variety of backgrounds, and each had their own reasons to leave home and to start a new life out west. Included are stories of life and death, attacks and pestilence, and even fashion." —Tamar Stone

work during the Crimean War. What she accomplished would change how nurses and the field of nursing would be considered from that point onward (both on the battlefield and at home). Many women were inspired by her work and joined the war as volunteers, following their husbands and brothers into the battlefields. Others disguised themselves as men in order to partake in the action on the front lines.

These stories include those told by author Louisa May Alcott in her book *Hospital Sketches*, published in 1863, before she wrote *Little Women*. They also include some stories of Sarah Emma Edmonds, also known as the soldier Franklin Flint Thompson, during the American Civil War. Their bed-oriented stories and experiences fill this folding army cot. The bag that that holds the bed and bedding is based on a design from military tent bags. The pie-chart design stitched on it is inspired by the "coxcomb" charts devised by Florence Nightingale to explain necessary health reforms, which she based on the mortality statistics of British army troops during the Crimean War.

Q: How did you start to commemorate your own romantic relationship through hooked rugs?

A: I didn't even consider the rugs as part of my artwork, but I guess they are! I My husband Bob and I decided to do a rug about our first three years together, before we got married in 2000. We talked about all the road-trip photos we took and food we ate and the souvenirs that we bought…and we made a list. Bob, who is an art director, sketched it out, and then I hooked the rug, which took me more than three years, while watching a lot of television. The strange thing was that neither of us noticed that the US map was actually backward,

Tamar Stone, *Our First 3 Years*, 2001, new and vintage wool, 69 x 47 in
(175.26 x 119.38 cm). Photo: Tamar Stone

Top: Stone, *H.T.W.E.* ("… *His Thanks Was Enough* …"), 2013, US military tent shelter, olive drab cotton sateen with two used olive drab Swedish military surplus straps and four metal buttons, embroidery, 20 x 27.5 in (50.8 x 69.85 cm). Photo: Tamar Stone

Bottom: Tamar Stone, tent bag components of *H.T.W.E.* ("…*His Thanks Was Enough*…"), 2013, including vintage cotton off-white mattress cover with inkjet printed image, vintage pillowcase ticking, cotton batting, vintage green army blanket, vintage brown wool blanket with two olive drab Swedish military surplus straps, 20 x 27.5 in (50.8 x 69.85 cm). Photo: Tamar Stone

as Florida was in the upper left corner. It didn't hit us until the whole thing was finished, though we kept thinking, Hmm, something looks funny.

Q: What do textiles allow you, as an artist who tells stories, to do that pen and paper don't?

A: Although I went to art school, I have to admit that I am not very good at drawing things. Even in school, I would prefer to collage images in order to get my point across, rather than put pencil to paper! I also enjoy using textiles because of the way they feel. And, whenever I can, I like to recycle by incorporating vintage textiles into the bedding material, as people did years ago when they couldn't afford to have a new mattress and they would stuff big cloth sacks or bags in order to sleep on them.

I use quotes from women who are well-known, but I also use stories from those who didn't become household names—their stories are just as important, and their voices should also be heard. I believe that it's vital to know where you came from in order to move forward in life, and there is a lot to be learned from the past. ✳

A TEXTILE TOME

Mohammad Mahir Hadri, a Syrian living in Dubai, has re-created the entire Quran using embroidered calligraphy, silk yarn, and velvet. His twelve-volume reproduction of the Quran contains 426 pages and weighs 440 lb (200 kg). It took him eight years to complete.

TRANSCRIPTION THROUGH CLOTH:

An Interview with Eleanor Hannan

Artist **Eleanor Hannan** and writer Elizabeth Dancoes have collaborated on several projects in which Elizabeth's words inspire Eleanor's machine embroidery and vice versa. Their work is a wonderful example of what happens when storytelling is not limited to the medium of paper and two artists work together to explore myth, creation, and culture.

Eleanor Hannan, page 23 of *1,001 Funny Things You Can Do with a Skirt*, 2011, machine embroidery on canvas, 9 x 12 in (22.86 x 30.48 cm). Photo: Ted Clark at Image This

Q: A collaboration between a writer and a textile artist doesn't happen very often. How did you and Elizabeth start to work together?

A: The idea for our project *1,001 Funny Things You Can Do with a Skirt* arose around 1995. Elizabeth and I met through a writer friend, and we were both interested in the new archaeology around the mythological figure of Baubo [an old woman in Greek mythology]. A number of books had been written about her, and she was beginning to appear as a significant presence in new theories about the ancient Greek myths. Through sourcing Baubo, we decided to collaborate to tell these intriguing stories of female power where the skirt is a vehicle of transformation. As collaborators, our ideas are anchored in our Baubo research and the ancient gesture called *ana suromai* (to raise the skirt) and its transformational implications. Originally, I began the work as pen drawings, but I felt I had to create an actual skirt that would be worn by a live model. I wanted to photograph it in order to get the color, look, and gestures I wanted for the stories.

We started with a set of four very short stories based on the lifting of the skirt. This imagery is surprisingly consistent throughout various cultural and mythological traditions and stories as a "change gesture." It even has resonances in the photo of Marilyn Monroe standing over a subway grate [with her skirt billowing]. We started with a set of stories based on ideas about the impact of the *ana suromai* gesture: a woman raising her skirt above her head with the right intention has the power to *Cow Bulls*, *Still Waves*, *Melt the Devil*, and *Defy Death*. The piece called *Knowing* is about cowing bulls.

We collected references from some of the ancient sources

Top & bottom: Eleanor Hannan, pages 8 and 12 of *1,001 Funny Things You Can Do with a Skirt*, 2011, machine embroidery on canvas, 9 x 12 in (22.86 x 30.48 cm). Photos: Ted Clark at Image This

and mythologies we read, interpreted them, and brought them together. Our first publicly shown piece was 4 x 6 inches [10.16 x 15.24 cm], the size of a postcard. Elizabeth wrote two paragraph-long stories that fit on one side. I embroidered densely colored, textured imagery for each line of her text. We left these out around the city as anonymous printed postcards.

Q: You often work in the mediums of drawing and photography. Why did you choose to use embroidery to tell these stories?

A: I had shifted my attention from drawing and works created on paper to free-motion embroidery. I used the sewing machine as a drawing tool. As I had stitched and embroidered all my life and had such passion for it, I was delighted by the challenge of exploring these very sensual, deeply figurative ideas through color and tonal, layered, hand-drawn machine stitching.

Q: How do you plan to illustrate a story using embroidery? Do you make the scenes one by one, or do you write the whole story prior to making the images?

A: We work on the ideas first. Then we both go away and do our thing. However, I would inevitably start on the drawings as soon as I had Elizabeth's text, and she worked from my image ideas. All of these components worked themselves out together—the stories, the text, the meaning and moral, the imagery, and the embroidery. Elizabeth's writing is beautiful, funny, sexy, and very concise. I read and re-read her writing, and then I start to sketch very simply. I evolve sketches to drawings for embroidery, then I prepare the

Eleanor Hannan, page 4 of *1,001 Funny Things You Can Do with a Skirt*, 2011, machine embroidery on canvas, 9 x 12 in (22.86 x 30.48 cm). Photo: Ted Clark at Image This

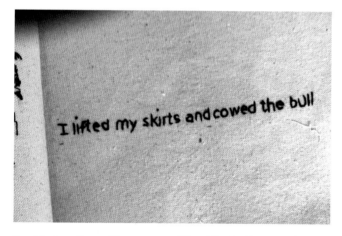

Top & bottom: Eleanor Hannan, pages 25 and 21 of *1,001 Funny Things You Can Do with a Skirt*, 2011, machine embroidery on canvas, 9 x 12 in (22.86 x 30.48 cm). Photos: Ted Clark at Image This

backgrounds and head into actually making the embroideries and storyboards, the captions and design. I interpret each of her lines, even sometimes each word-sense, so there are so many more drawings than there are lines of text.

Q: What are the unique challenges to making stories out of textiles?

A: Creating a book out of textiles is labor-intensive and the creations are one-of-a-kind. There are also design decisions about how the pages will be read or seen. Where do the captions go? Should I use captions or whole sentences? There are material choices. Should I use super-thick canvas and embroidery floss or paper, and how can I deal with floppiness and fraying? We deal with decisions around the book as "object," such as what to do with the back of each page, and how best to stitch on so small an object. And, how do we sell it? I imposed all of these questions on myself, but I had one wonderful summer embroidering it.

Q: What are you working on now?

A: I am working on the imagery for Elizabeth's *Silly Skirt Poem*, which I will show in the next two years. I am also creating a revised version of *Lunch*. This material is rich and profound, and it will inspire us until the end of our working lives. Our next project will be re-evaluating the implications of the lifted skirt gesture from our now-older perspectives. The passion with which we started has evolved, and so has the relevance of the ideas. Artistically, I love sharing this compelling and complex truth through stitching and humor. ✳

Prompt

The Button Jar

Having trouble coming up with new ideas? Try this writing prompt. All you need is a pen, some paper, and a collection of buttons.

Spend some time alone with a button collection—your own or one belonging to someone else. Pour all of the buttons onto a flat surface. Ask yourself the following questions, and answer them in writing:

- If each button had an emotion, what would it be?

- If each button had a name, what would it be?
  TIP: Don't think too hard, just write down the first thing that comes to mind.

- Which button reminds you of an important time in your life? Why?

- Close your eyes. Which button feels best to the touch? Why?

- Is there a button that you don't like? What causes this reaction?

- What sort of party would these buttons have gone to together? Who would have worn them?

- If one button was the "leader" of all of the other buttons, who would it be? Why?

YOU DON'T HAVE TO STITCH IT

There are a wide variety of ways to render typefaces on cloth. Each of these techniques requires its own tools and unique skills, but taking the time to learn even one of them will expand your crafting repertoire.

- Embroidery: Draw designs onto cloth with a disappearing ink pen, chalk dressmaker's pencil, or carbon trace paper before tracing them with your stitching.

- Cross-stitch: Design your typeface on grid paper, and use this as a guide when transferring your design to even-weave fabric.

- Machine embroidery: Many digital embroidery machines can read a computer graphic. You can also try to freehand the text. Remember that practice makes perfect.

- Intarsia or Fair Isle knitting: Your local yarn store may give classes on these graphic techniques.

- Felting: Felt roving or 100-percent wool yarn can be applied in script to a pure felt base, then felted into place by hand using a felting needle.

- Photo transfer: While not waterproof, images can be applied to fabric with a blender marker/pen. Using a carbon-heavy photocopy of the text (reversed so that it does not read mirror-image when transferred), place the image face-down on the fabric. Saturate the back of the image with a blender pen, taking care not to shift the image. Burnish the paper using the back of a spoon, evenly rubbing it across the image area. When you lift the paper, you should have a perfect image transfer.

- Appliqué: Cut letters from pieces of fabric and adhere to a background with a simple straight stitch or a blanket stitch.

- Silkscreen and ink blocking: Speedball Art (*speedballart.com* or at most art supply stores) sells a variety of kits with all the tools you need to get started silkscreening or creating block prints.

LITTLE TOKENS:

An Interview with Maria Damon

Maria Damon is chair of the Humanities and Media Studies Department at the Pratt Institute's School of Liberal Arts and Science. A literary scholar, she self-identifies as a folk-artist and closeted writer and poet who happily hasn't "kept it in the closet very well." In addition to weaving, embroidery, and collaborations with other artists in her textile work, Maria also has a blog called *Text, Textile, Exile* that explores "the matrices of text, textile, and exile through metaphor, networks, poetics, etymologies, etc., with an occasional subplot relating these elements to Iggy and the Stooges." hyperpoesia.net

Maria Damon, *X(exoxial)-stitch*, 2000, cross-stitch on evenweave cloth, 6.5 x 12 in (16.51 x 30.48 cm). Photo: Jeff T. Johnson

Q: How did you get into weaving?

A: In 1969, the summer of Woodstock, I was fourteen years old and very sulky. I think my mother was at her wit's end, so she signed my sister and me up for some craft classes. The pottery didn't take, but the weaving did. I had a blissful time that summer.

In the fall, when I returned to school, my parents got me a Nilus Leclerc loom, which I still have. Marguerite Davison's *A Handweaver's Pattern Book* was very big in the 1970s. It was a guide to weaving with a focus on Appalachian patterns, and it became my bible. There was something magical about the names of the patterns, such as "Whitman's Fancy," or "The Rose of Sharon." They were like mini-narratives themselves.

Q: You've gifted some of your handmade items to musicians and notable artists. Others have responded to your pieces with some writing. Can you tell me about this exchange?

A: I've always made these little things—I call them tokens—but about fifteen years ago, I started one with the intermedia poet, publisher, and cultural anarchist mIEKAL aND. He has a press called Xexoxial Editions, and I made him a little X-E-X-O-X-E cross-stitch with different alphabet patterns from sampler books, from old Scottish to Modern. The second token was for Rita Raley, a colleague of mine at the University of Minnesota who works on electronic poetry and poetics. She wrote a piece called *Reveal Codes*. There's a command that reveals the code underlying an algorithm, which enables you to generate text. *Reveal Codes* is a very resonant, poetic, and even mystical phrase that also has technological significance. Within that phrase are the words

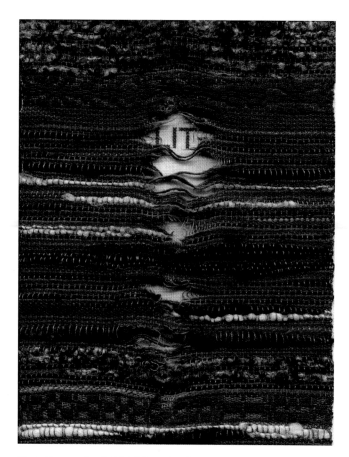

Maria Damon, detail of *Ed Cohen's Scarf*, 1997, approximately 7 ft x 7 in (2.13 m x 17.78 cm). Photo: Jeff T. Johnson

"real ode," so I made this little piece called *Reveal Codes: Real Ode for Reality*, i.e., Rita Raley, with a little computer on the side.

I started giving pieces to literary friends that had significance both to me and to the recipient. It's become my practice, and it feels to me as if a piece is incomplete if it doesn't end up with someone. It's kind of like a rarefied, sublimated version of making a sweater for a boyfriend—you don't invest the energy in making something unless you're emotionally engaged.

Q: Is creating a piece of writing in response to something and creating a textile piece the same experience?

A: It's easier and more intuitive for me to respond with color and with elements that don't necessarily use sophisticated language but focus on one or two puns or words with multiple levels of meaning embedded in them. It's also true that once you start using words professionally, there's a performance anxiety that develops around it. This was my way of taking notes and processing material.

Q: You also created some woven white silk scarves for literary spirits, including one for beat poet Allen Ginsberg. Did you do that when he was alive?

A: Yes, I made that in 1995 or 1996. In the course of being a poetry person myself, I had been around him quite a bit, but it's not like he knew who I was. I had studied at institutions he taught at, I sat in on his classes, I went to parties at his apartment—but I wasn't really in his orbit. When I was teaching at the University of Minnesota, he came through Minneapolis, and I made him a white silk scarf and

Allen Ginsberg wearing a white scarf woven and gifted to him by Maria Damon, City Lights Bookstore, San Francisco, 1997. Photo: Chris Felver

Maria Damon, *Derek's Stooges Scarf*, 2012, cross-stitch on hand woven scarf, 7 ft x 7 in (2.13 m x 17.78 cm). Photo: Jeff T. Johnson

presented it to him. Then I saw him again at the Naropa Institute, and I mentioned the scarf to him, not expecting him to remember it. He said, "Oh, yes! I had this for quite a while." I thought he was just being polite, but a couple of years ago I saw a book of photographs of the beat poets in their later years, and there was a photo of him wearing the scarf I made him and looking kind of rabbinical. Seeing the photo was really emotional and wonderful for me.

I made another scarf for the Caribbean poet Edward Kamau Braithwaite. I also got into making black scarves for the Stooges. They are black with red cross-stitch.

Q: On your blog you post poetic explorations of different textile-related words, such as skein, warp, and weft. Can you tell me more about that?

A: Like a lot of poets, I'm obsessed with etymology. I started to think about text and textile. They are from the same etymological origins. In the world in which I move professionally, textile practices are used as metaphors for textual practices. People will say, "She wove a narrative." Particularly in the 1980s and early '90s, a lot of feminist literary scholars were using these phrases because textile production was considered a feminine domestic enterprise. A lot of feminist literary scholars would use weaving or sewing metaphors to structure their papers, but inadvertently revealed that they knew absolutely nothing about the actual processes of weaving. For example, they wouldn't realize that you would start weaving at one end and work your way down or that weaving a tapestry isn't the same as sewing a dress, or that crocheting or knitting are completely different processes than weaving or embroidery. They thought using textile metaphors would emphasize their status as women writing about women writers.

What I realized was that text and textile are not metaphors for each other; they are the same thing. Paleo-linguist Elizabeth Barber studies ancient languages and textiles, and she points out that the same tools used for writing were used for making shelter and clothing—the quill dipped in ink is the same as the needle; parchment or skin for writing was also used to make shelters; and the inner bark of a tree was used not only to create material for clothing or canoes, but was also something to write upon. The textile was not a primitive foreshadowing of the text to come. The text people think that textiles are just a linguistic resource for them, primitive materials that they're going to bring to fruition with their brilliant insights. But, in fact, they're inseparable.

Q: Tell me about the *(Asemic) Raw Power/Power* scarf.

A: There's a form of visual poetry that is called asemic writing; it looks like writing, but it can't be read. When I was posting pictures on the blog, I would post the front side of an embroidery and the reverse side. The reverse side is the asemic side, because you can kind of tell what it says; it's sort of writing, but it's sort of not. Tony Trehy, curator and founder of the Text Festival in Bury, England, saw this piece online and was interested in displaying it with the emphasis on the reverse side. It was an eye-opener for me. I get two visual poems for the price of one by using the front and the reverse sides and giving them two different names. One is *Kill City*; the other is *Asemic Kill City*.

Maria Damon, *Open Up and Bleed*, 2008, cross-stitch on evenweave cloth, approximately 5 x 6 in (12.7 x 15.24 cm). Photo: Jeff T. Johnson

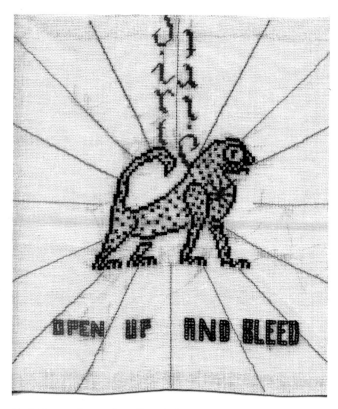

Maria Damon, *Streetwalking Cheetah: for Natalie Schlossman*, 2013, cross-stitch on evenweave cloth, 9.5 x 9.5 in (24.13 x 24.13 cm). Photo: Jeff T. Johnson

Q: What are you working on now?

A: I am working on a series of collaborations with a poet I've never met, and they all seem to have a sea theme. There's a whole community of visual poets working with asemic writing or with the alphabet. Some people say it's like typography or graphic design, and there's overlap, but it's a wide community. I'm happy that they have embraced me. Somehow I've managed to merge my interests in poetry and textiles in a way that combines the very primitive with the avant-garde. It feels almost like a miracle that it's crystallized in such an easy, happy way. ✳

Chapter Two

THE STORIES WE WEAR

Fashion is not something that exists in dresses only. Fashion is in the sky, in the street. Fashion has to do with ideas, the way we live, what is happening.

—Coco Chanel

Our clothing

My winter coat was black leather, beaten and soft, long and cinched in the middle, hooded and fur-lined. It got compliments everywhere I went. It became something of a legend in my friendship circle and a symbol of me to my closet friends. Then I was hit by a car. The leather coat protected me from gravel rash. It was cut away as I lay unconscious in emergency. My best friend was the first to my bedside. She saw the shreds of my coat and said that it filled her with fear and grief; its rips and tears were indicative of my injuries, its pieces were like my broken body.

—Bonnie Abbott

Once when I was a scruffy teen, I tried on a lavender grad dress that was so femme-y and grownup that I felt physically dizzy when I looked at myself. My body looked fine, but the style was so far from my usual way of presenting myself that it gave me the spins.

—Kat Siddle

In the back of my closet hangs a light blue cardigan sweater. It belonged to my beloved Gramps. The sweater matched his blue eyes, and he wore it for many years. I learned everything I know about living with grace and courage while experiencing chronic illness and disability from him. After multiple strokes, he often struggled with small motor skills such as doing up the buttons on the sweater. Once he had put the sweater on, he'd come and stand silently in front of me, and that was my cue to button him up. After he died, the nursing home packed up his things. Summer came, and I decided it was time to deal with them. I stood there with tears running down my face. It seemed so sad to me that such a great man's life had been reduced to two small suitcases. When I opened them, I found his blue sweater. Every now and then, when I am pulling something from my closet, I see it and touch it. If we ever had a fire at our home, it would be one of the few things I would try to save.

—Lelainia Lloyd

It is impossible to explore the juxtaposition between textiles and storytelling without a nod to the textiles that we know most intimately, our clothing. Clothing is part of our lives, from our first moments when we are swaddled in soft cloth by our mothers to the formal dress that we wear at the ceremonies that acknowledge life's important passages. What we wear can mark our financial and social status, religion, political affiliations, and nationalities. High school letter jackets, employee uniforms, fan hockey jerseys, tutus, caftans, yoga pants, grad dresses, hoodies, christening gowns, or combat fatigues—our garments help to shape our identities.

Let the work of the artists in this chapter invite you to think about the role of clothing in your own life—what do the things you choose to wear say about you? Do garments that you own make you remember the past? Has your clothing changed your life in any way? How does clothing allow you to look forward to the future?

Clothing not only keeps us warm and protects our skin, it is how we interact with one another and our environment. The clothes we wear possess the means to conjure memories, incite personal transformation, and express our aspirations.

Once a year we'd get new shoes. One year, my brothers and I got cowboy boots, and we became tough, kicking the ground and swearing. Another year, we got new running shoes, and we would run everywhere, thinking we were faster just for wearing them.

—Jordan Mitchell

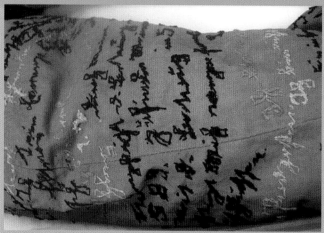

Top: Agnes Richter, jacket, c. 1895, embroidery on cotton straightjacket, Prinzhorn Collection, University of Heidelberg, Germany. Photo: Liz Aldag

Bottom: Detail of Agnes Richter's jacket. Photo: Liz Aldag

Clothing in the Asylum

For those who have faced internment, textiles can offer an escape. In the mid-1890s, Agnes Richter, a former seamstress and patient at an Austrian psychiatric asylum, created a woman's jacket out of her institutional uniform. This jacket was embellished inside and out with her own life story.

Agnes's embroidered writing was so profuse that much of the text is hard to discern; words disappear into different strands of thread and emerge from unrelated phrases. In this untamed writing, one can catch the odd declarative snippet: "my jacket," or "my white stockings." Agnes transformed a sterile garment into something that is deeply personal, emotional, and also obsessive.

The jacket is part of the Prinzhorn Collection at the University in Heidelberg, which holds more than 5,000 works created by patients in psychiatric hospitals in the late nineteenth and early twentieth centuries.

PSYCHOLOGIST

Gail A. Hornstein's book *Agnes's Jacket: A Psychologist's Search for the Meaning of Madness* is an attempt to decode the markings on the garment she likened to a "hieroglyph before the discovery of the Rosetta Stone."

Clothing for Remembrance

Sometimes the very act of creating something from a piece clothing can bring us closer to the person who wore it. Dealing with the devastating effects of Alzheimer's disease on her mother's personality, artist Anne Montgomery turned to stitching on her mother's wedding dress:

"I had planned to slowly destroy her dress as I moved from the front to the back, but when I first started to stitch, I realized that what I wanted was to celebrate my mother, not [focus on] the disease."

The work-in-progress is decorated with her mother's name in a historically accurate font. Montgomery plans to add photo transfers and real photographs to the dress. She writes: "As I stitch, I think of my mom and who she was at those particular periods in her life. It's a relaxing way to think about her."

....

Top right: Anne Montgomery, *My Mother's Dress*, embroidery and photo transfer on her mother's wedding dress, dimensions unknown, work in progress. Photo: Anne Montgomery

Bottom right: Anne Montgomery, detail of *My Mother's Dress*. Photo: Anne Montgomery

CLOTHING AS SOCIAL HISTORY:
An Interview with Rosalind Wyatt

Calligrapher and textile artist Rosalind Wyatt's *The Stitched Lives of Others* has been compared to a modern Bayeux Tapestry. A work in progress, the tapestry will consist of 215 garments that represent the lives of Londoners; the number of garments equals the length of the river Thames in miles. The project began in 2011 when Rosalind stitched on a pair of Edwardian silk dancing shoes that represented Mary Pearse, the daughter of a shoemaker. Replicating handwriting with her needle, Rosalind stitched Mary's 1815 admittance record to a poorhouse after she ran away from home. Rosalind is creating a history of her city in textile by meticulously stitching the recollected lives of others.

Q: What brought you, as a writer and bookbinder, to embroidery?

A: My first degree was in calligraphy and bookbinding. I always wanted to push the boundaries and experiment with writing using different tools. While studying at the Royal College of Art, I started to research original documents at the British Library, purely for their visual aesthetic qualities. I thought, maybe I could write with a needle. I taught myself. I see the thread as the line. I draw it with my needle and thread—there's nothing pre-printed or drawn beforehand. That would kill the spontaneity of the mark.

Q: Your project *The Stitch Lives of London* series sounds very ambitious—having 215 stitched garments stretch the length of the River Thames! What inspired it?

A: After I created *The Stitch Lives of Others*, people kept approaching me with their stories and textiles. I suppose they felt I was a vehicle to tell their story, and inevitably I felt there was a larger story to tell. As I am a born and bred Londoner, it had to be about London, which is an endlessly inspiring place to live and work. It will not be a literal, narrative commentary on the history of London—it's more about placing the "voices" or garments side by side and seeing what effect that has. After all, that's how we live— side by side, breathing the same air, with the same desires and fears.

Rosalind Wyatt, *I Wish I Were with You*, 2013, satin, lace, and embroidery, approximately 35.43 x 35.43 in (90 x 90 cm). Photo: mlrphoto.com. This commissioned project explores, through letters and receipts, Winston Churchill's love of shopping at [London department store] Fortnum & Mason.

Q: What is the balance of contemporary versus historical in your work? How much is factual and how much is personal interpretation?

A: Until Doreen Lawrence, the mother of murdered teenager Stephen Lawrence, donated a garment to *The Stitch Lives of London*, all the pieces were historical. History is all about personal interpretation; for instance, most Londoners have followed the Stephen Lawrence story and lived through the harrowing details of the case. [Lawrence, a young black man, was murdered in a racist attack in 1993 while waiting for a bus.] Most have a personal and highly politicized opinion about it. However, when I met Doreen, all that seemed irrelevant. Through our dialogue, it was clear that the piece would celebrate his life rather than mourn his death. I hope that *A Boy Who Loved to Run* offers hope, and that this will be carried on in the work that Doreen continues to do. It is a social commentary on an event in our city's history. ✳

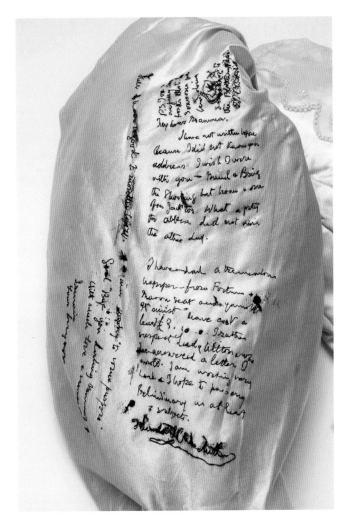

Rosalind Wyatt, detail of *I Wish I Were with You*, 2013. This letter written by sixteen-year-old Winston Churchill to his mother is stitched on a satin and whale bone bodice. Photo: mlrphoto.com

STORIES TO RATTLE YOUR BONES:
An Interview with Teresa Burrows

Teresa Burrows is an award-winning artist who lives in Thompson, Manitoba. Born in England, she grew up in Vancouver and Winnipeg before moving to northern Manitoba. Trained as a printmaker and a painter, Teresa applies her expressive glass beading to wall hangings and sculptural clothing. Not one to shy away from strong subject matter, Teresa's work explores aspects of violence, oppression, mental illness, female vulnerability, and strength. Her techniques and work are influenced by her experience living in Canada's north. *glassartcanada.ca/public/artist/Teresa.Burrows#portfolio*

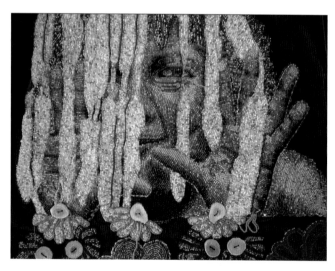

Teresa Burrows, detail of *Caribou Woman (madre primavera)*, 2008–2009, beadwork, fur, dimensions unknown. Photo: Teresa Burrows

Q: It is impossible to see your work and not think about where you live. What's it like in northern Manitoba?

A: When I moved north, an Aboriginal family adopted me. I was welcomed into many of the cultural traditions that other non-Aboriginal peoples might not experience. Later, I was hired to work at the Ma-Mow-We-Tak Friendship Centre in Thompson, Manitoba, as cultural programmer. I learned from the elders there. One elder, Cecelia Donaldson, taught me how to do beadwork, though I didn't use this skill until much later.

I married someone from the north, and we have raised our three children there. I worked as a probation officer and addictions counselor, but I started to suffer from back problems and had to have two surgeries. My physiotherapist and chiropractor encouraged me to return to painting to increase my mobility, so I quit working and started painting full-time, large paintings about four by eight feet [1.22 x 2.43 m]. I also studied at the University of Manitoba as a printmaker. I would do photo shoots with models and props in order to create reference materials for my paintings, but slowly I began to see the photographs as art. By that time, I was creating handmade props, and I started to see that they were actually art. Eventually, the photography became about documentation, and the paintings never happened.

Q: Can you tell me about the *(a)las in rupertsland* series?

A: I am married to a Hudson, and I live in the original Hudson's Bay Company fur trade area [which was known as Rupert's Land]. I wanted to do a version of *Alice in Wonderland* in which Alice is taken from her English lands and brought into the fur trade. I took themes within the Alice stories and re-interpreted them through themes of colonization. The beaver pelt was a big part of why the English, French, and First Nations made contact and how Canada was built as a nation. That contact didn't always happen on good terms, hence the title, *a(las) in rupertsland*. In creating this series, I revisited characters from *Alice in Wonderland* in the context of the history of contact and the exploitation of people. I made Mad Hatter hats on vintage beaver felt. The chemicals used in producing these hats, specifically mercury vapors, poisoned the makers and made them insane. I created a Sulfur Queen figure, a flip side of the British Queen, the great mother of the treaties. The series also features a mock turtle who sings sadly about his residential school days.

THE HUDSON'S BAY COMPANY

is a department store that originated in 1670 as a fur-trading company and outpost in British North America, or what is now Canada and the United States. The company relied heavily on trade relationships with First Nations and Native American tribes. Wool blankets, known as Hudson's Bay point blankets, were traded for beaver pelts and other furs during the seventeenth and eighteenth centuries. Point blankets were valued by First Nations and given to respected elders at potlatches and community celebrations. These blankets are still coveted by collectors, and while some see them as a symbol of Canada's history, others identify them with an incident in which they may have been used to spread smallpox in a First Nations community.

Teresa Burrows, *the sul(fur) queen* from the *(a)las in rupertsland* series, 2007, fur, beadwork, Hudson Bay blanket, beaver skulls, dimensions unknown. Photo: Teresa Burrows

Top (left & right): Teresa Burrows, *Caribou Woman in Her Flowers Ceremonial Robe*, 2010, beadwork, cloth, antlers, dimensions unknown. Photo: Teresa Burrows

Q: What are you referencing in the series *Caribou Women*?

A: Many northern peoples have similar stories about the sun, the reindeer, and the caribou. The reindeer return the sun to the north each spring, carrying it on their antlers on their migration to their birthing grounds. The matron female [of the herd] leads the pregnant reindeer north first. First Nations have many ceremonies for the return of the sun and to ward off spirits who cause mental illness during the long, isolating winters. This work was about the power of women; you have the power to shine at any point in your life.

Q: Tell me about *blue beaver's burden* and *the disappearance of the shaking tent sisters*.

A: After the light, there is the dark. *Pro Pelle Cutem* (Latin for "a skin for a skin") is the Hudson's Bay Company's motto; [it is interpreted to mean that the early fur traders] risked their lives for skins, i.e., pelts. I decided to look at women and how they risk their lives with skin, whether intentionally in the sex trade or unintentionally because their gender makes them vulnerable. *Blue beaver's burden* and *the disappearance of the shaking tent sisters* is about murdered and missing women in Manitoba and some of society's attitudes about violence, women, and the sex trade.

The piece called *Hide* continued this theme as I looked at child sexual exploitation. [Abused] children hide in shame or add another "skin" to deal with their lives. *Hide* was based on the sexual abuse that my own mother experienced between the ages of two and sixteen, on the story of a young woman in the north who was impregnated by her grandfather, and on the many young boys sexually abused by convicted sex offender Ralph Knight Rowe, who was an Anglican minister, Boy Scout leader, foster parent, and pilot. I was his probation officer. Later, as an addictions counselor I met many of his victims at a treatment center; they hid their shame in alcohol and drugs.

I am presently completing new works for *she's come undone*, a series about motherhood, mental illness, and the madness and mysteries that women make of their lives. This new series will look at choices women make. One story is about Isabel Gunn, an Orkney girl who dressed as a man so she could work in the fur trade, until she was discovered in labor. She was returned to the Orkneys, where it was said that she made a meager living knitting socks and mittens for fishermen and dockhands and died in poverty. ✳

Teresa Burrows, *secrets of the skin room*, 2012, bearskin robe, beadwork, cloth, metal, dimensions unknown. Photo: Teresa Burrows

TRANSFORMATIVE CLOTHING IN LITERATURE

In the world of writing, clothing often has the ability to become a transformative item. From the Big Bad Wolf dressing up like Little Red Riding Hood's grandmother to Harry Potter's Cloak of Invisibility, garments have long been used as devices by storytellers.

- Set in London in the year 1748, Emma Donoghue's historical novel *Slammerkin* tells of a clothing-obsessed protagonist, led into prostitution by the promise of a shiny red ribbon. She lives by three rules: 1. Never give up your liberty, 2. Clothes make the woman, and 3. Clothes are the greatest lie ever told.

- In Agatha Christie's detective novel *The Man in the Brown Suit*, the characters speculate about the identity of the man in the brown suit. (And Christie's Miss Marple is not only a detective but a committed knitter.)

- In Ann Brashares' popular series of young adult novels *The Sisterhood of the Traveling Pants*, a transformative pair of jeans is passed among a group of young women, securing their friendships and interlacing four coming-of-age stories.

- Science fiction master Philip K. Dick created "scramble suits" in his book *A Scanner Darkly*. Scramble suits confuse the senses and make the wearer indescribable and unrecognizable—a perfect plot device to foil an interrogation.

- In Roch Carrier's children's book *The Hockey Sweater*, the protagonist's mother replaces his too-small jersey with one in the colors of the rival team. Conflict ensues.

CONFESSIONAL COUTURE:
An Interview with Noël Palomo-Lovinski

Noël Palomo-Lovinski is a wife, mother, and professor at the Fashion School at Kent State University in Ohio. Her artistic work includes a series of couturier-inspired gowns digitally printed with phrases taken from sensationalist talk shows, banal celebrity newscasts, and internet chat rooms. Her work raises questions of transparency, honesty, and social exchanges in our new digital reality. Noël is the author of *The World's Most Influential Fashion Designers: Hidden Connections and Lasting Legacies of Fashion's Iconic Creators.*

Noël Palomo-Lovinski, detail of *Bridezilla*, 2009, digitally printed tulle with fiber-reactive dye on pearls, 106 x 44 in (269.24 x 111.76 cm). Photo: Noël Palomo-Lovinski

Q: What is the story behind your project *Confessions*?

A: When my kids were very little, I was learning to negotiate the demands of life as a mother, a wife, and a professional who was going through tenure, a process that demands an extreme level of directed self-scrutiny. I was reading blogs and other confessional websites, and I became attracted to ones that related to what it means to be a woman in today's society; I noticed that a lot of my friends were experiencing similar issues and feelings as those reflected by women posting on these websites. *Confessions* is made up of a series of twelve gowns covered with phrases from the sites. Some of the quotes are my own; they reflect how I felt. One of the gowns is hand-embroidered, and the rest are made up of digitally printed fabrics.

Q: Writer and textile artist Mary Smull described your work as "evoking complex relationships—of the self to the public, of viewer to voyeur—in a social-networking age."

A: Our sense of community, and how it is formed, has changed dramatically with the advent of the internet. Our media-centric society, coupled with the importance of the talk show throughout the 1990s, has influenced a trend to relate to others by watching and personalizing their experiences. There is a tense negotiation between what is private and what is public and open for judgment. While this dynamic has always been present in culture, it is compounded by social networking.

Noël Palomo-Lovinski, *All Tied Up in Knots*, 2009, digitally printed duchess satin, 66 x 18 in (167.64 x 45.72 cm). Photo: Noël Palomo-Lovinski

Q: I've read that you have a fascination with the sensationalist nature of talk shows and the fact that they often feature women making intimate confessions. How do these confessions play into your artwork?

A: It is the act of confession—the baring of one's soul and the sense of intimacy, or false intimacy—that is so interesting to me. Women bond through emotions. Shared experience is not limited to a geographic area now that we have confessional websites and television.

As a naturally reserved person, I noticed a long time ago that if I don't divulge anything about myself, I have a harder time being accepted by other women. Women demand that social interaction connect to a sense of vulnerability in some way. Clothing is connected to these ideas since it helps the wearer convey messages about who they are, what they believe in, and what perception they want you to take away from them. Clothing marks identity, just as confessions do. Does putting confessions onto clothing change the meaning of these phrases? Not really. In a sense, clothing becomes the broadcast system. I try to shape the silhouette of each gown to convey an abstracted idea of the words so that there is a narrative throughout in the words and in the form of each dress.

Q: Tell me about *All Tied Up in Knots*.

A: I was interested in the dichotomy between "letting it all out" and keeping one's feelings penned in. It is common wisdom that emotions need to be expressed to be resolved, but that often becomes tricky if someone's feelings are hurt. I was interested in confessions that were about the suppression of feelings or the inability to communicate. The only alternative for many women was to let off steam on an anonymous website. The text is in pink and purple—saccharine, traditionally feminine colors—to reference the idea that women are often expected to be peaceable and not ruffle any feathers. The armor is about holding in feelings that "leak out" anyway.

Q: What is the story behind *Sucker Punch*?

A: The text begins as benign on the top layer. The second layer has matching quotes that are somewhat unexpected in their cruelty or ferocity. This is again about the suppression of feelings in a face-to-face environment and confession of true thoughts on an anonymous blog. The shoulder harness is a reference to making oneself bigger—how women stand taller when they wear shoulder pads. Confessing and being allowed to be "snarky" or nasty—not desirable feminine traits, but ones which are often part of the feminine social system—made the confessors feel bolder or stronger.

Q: What inspired *Bridezilla*?

A: I found a website called *Bridezilla*. It surprised me how many brides felt angry, hurt, and overwhelmed. I'm a child of the 1980s, and it reminded me of how both the wedding of Lady Diana and Prince Charles and the demise of their marriage was made public. The public got whipped up about the importance of fairy-tale weddings. The dress itself was inspired by Diana, and the quotes, which are in bubble-gum pink, are confessions from real "bridezillas". I intentionally made the print small so people need to lean in close to read it. I enjoy watching the look of shock on their faces as the less-than-flattering quotes are read.

Noël Palomo-Lovinski, *Sucker Punch*, 2009, digitally printed silk chiffon, duchess satin, 80 x 16 in (203.2 x 40.64 cm). Photo: Noël Palomo-Lovinski

Noël Palomo-Lovinski, *Bridezilla*, 2009, digitally printed tulle with fiber-reactive dye on pearls, 106 x 44 in (269.24 x 111.76 cm). Photo: Noël Palomo-Lovinski

Q: Are there any misconceptions about your work?

A: A lot of people get the impression that I am terribly depressed or have a terrible husband or something after reading some of these confessions. They think that these are personal. I have a wonderful husband and I am very happy! My work is about female bonding. It's about confessing the pressures and concerns that people feel in an abstracted and chaotic digital age, and how they choose to feel better. ✳

Prompt

In Your Closet

This easy prompt will get you thinking about the clothes in your closet using only the sensation of touch.

To begin, close your eyes and run your hand through the clothes hanging in your closet. Rest your hand on an item that feels interesting. Don't look at it. Turn away and answer the following questions in writing. Devote a full paragraph to each question.

- What did it feel like?
- What did it remind you of?
- Where did you wear it?
- How did you come by it?
- Why is it important?

Now look at the items in your closet. Can you locate which garment you wrote about? Does looking change your responses to the questions? Try answering your questions anew. See what changes for you in the response.

Project

Close to the Heart: A Memory Sweater

BRIFRISCHU

Inspired by her late grandmother, brifrishu's pattern for this lovely little raglan sweater keeps the things that are nearest and dearest to us close.

"This sweater has been a way for me to reconnect with my late grandmother's history. She developed dementia in her later life and moved in with my parents. Her relationship with her husband, who died quite suddenly, had been something she always was proud of. So, even when it seemed that she slipped away day by day, the time she had spent with my grandfather was a source of consolation to her. It was what she remembered and spoke of most. For me, it has become the thing to remember her by: the shy smile in her wedding photo, a love letter from my grandfather, and her wedding ring. With this sweater, I am able to carry them close to my heart, for everyone to see, so that I can share the memories, the words, and the stories behind them."

FINISHED MEASUREMENTS

Bust: 34 (38, 42, 46) in (86.5 cm [96.5, 106.5, 117] cm)
Length: 19.5 (20, 21, 22) in (49 [51, 53, 56] cm)
Sleeve width: 11 (12, 13.5, 14.5) in (27.5 [31, 34.5, 37] cm)

TOOLS & MATERIALS

- 900 (1050, 1200, 1350) yd (825 [960, 1100, 1240] m) DK weight wool yarn (121 yd [110 m] per 1.76 oz [50 g])

- 218 yd (200 m) DK weight linen or cotton yarn

- 1 spool invisible sewing thread

- US 6/4 mm knitting needles or size needed to obtain gauge

- US 0/2 mm knitting needles

- E/3.5 mm crochet hook

- darning needle

- materials to place in your pockets. This project uses a wedding ring, a family photograph, and a hand-written letter, but you could use anything that is meaningful to your own story.

GAUGE

23 sts & 28 rows = 4 in (10 cm) stockinette stitch

SKILLS

basic knitting

basic crochet

finish sewing

PATTERN NOTES

Knitting abbreviations:

RS: right side of work

WS: wrong side of work

k: knit

k1: knit one stitch

kfb: knit into the front and back of the stitch

p: purl

p1: purl one stitch

ssk: slip slip knit

sts: stitches

k2tog: knit together

Stockinette stitch:

    Row 1 (RS): knit

    Row 2 (WS): purl

If you wish to add depth in the back, work 3–4 sets of short rows, shaping before working the last set of decreases for the sweater back.

☞ Front

Using main yarn and larger knitting needles, cast on 98 (110, 120, 132) sts.

Waist Decreases:
Rows 1–7: Work stockinette stitch.
Row 8 (RS): K1, ssk, knit to last 3 sts, k2tog, k1.

Repeat rows 1–8 until piece measures 5 (5, 5.5, 5.5) in (12.5 [12.5, 14, 14] cm) from cast on edge, ending after working a RS row.

Waist Increases:
Rows 1–7: Work stockinette stitch.
Row 8 (RS): K1, kfb, knit to last 2 sts, kfb, k1.

Repeat rows 1–8 until piece measures 10 (10, 11, 11) in (25.5 [25.5, 28, 28] cm) from cast on edge.

Work even in stockinette stitch until piece measures 14 (14, 15, 16) in (35.5 [35.5, 38, 40.5] cm) from cast on edge, ending after working WS row.

Shoulder shaping:
Cast off 2 sts, work until end of row. Repeat on following row.

Row 1 (RS): K1, k2tog, knit to end of row.
Row 2 (WS): P1, p2tog, purl to end of row.
Repeat Rows 1 and 2 until 66 (72, 86, 96) sts remain.

Neck shaping:
Row 1: K1, ssk, k 13 [14, 20, 21], bind off 34 [38, 40, 48], knit to 3 sts before end of row, k2tog, k1.

Right shoulder:
Row 1 (WS): P1, p2tog, purl to end of row.
Row 2 (RS): cast off 2 sts, knit until end of row.
Repeat Row 1 and Row 2 2 [2, 3, 3] more times.
Next row (WS): P1, p2tog, purl until end of row. Bind off loosely.

Left shoulder:
Rejoin yarn, ready to work RS row.
Row 1 (RS): K1, k2tog, knit to end of row.
Row 2 (WS): Cast off 2 sts, purl to end of row.
Repeat rows 1 and 2 two more times.
Next row (RS): K1, k2tog, knit to end of row.
Work 1 row even. Bind off loosely.

☞ Back

Using main yarn and larger knitting needles, cast on 98 [110, 120, 132] sts.

Waist Decreases:
Rows 1–7: Work stockinette stitch.
Row 8 (RS): K1, ssk, knit to last 3 sts, k2tog, k1.

Repeat rows 1–8 until piece measures 5 (5, 5.5, 5.5) in (12.5 [12.5, 14, 14] cm) from cast on edge, ending after working a RS row.

Waist Increases:
Rows 1–7: Work stockinette stitch.
Row 8 (RS): K1, kfb, knit until 2 sts before the end of the row, kfb, k1.

Repeat rows 1–8 until piece measures 10 (10, 11, 11) in (25.5 [25.5, 28, 28] cm) from cast on edge.

Work evenly in stockinette stitch until piece measures 14 (14, 15, 16) in (35.5 [35.5, 38, 40.5] cm) from cast on edge, ending after working WS row.

Shoulder shaping:
Cast off 2 sts, work until end of row. Repeat on following row.

Row 1 (RS): K1, k2tog, knit to end of row.
Row 2 (WS): P1, p2tog, purl to end of row.
Repeat rows 1 and 2 until 66 (72, 86, 96) sts remain.

If desired, work 2–3 sets of short rows to add extra height to the back of the sweater.

Row 1 (RS): K1, ssk, knit to last 3 sts, k2tog, k1.
Row 2 (WS): Purl all stitches.
Repeat last 2 rows 2 (2, 3, 3) more times. Knit one row even. Bind off all stitches loosely.

☞ Sleeve

Knit 2 using main yarn and larger needles.

Cast on 62 (70, 78, 84) sts.
Work 17 (9, 5, 5) rows of stockinette stitch.
Next row (RS): k1, ssk, k to last 3 sts, k2tog, k1.

Repeat last 18 (10, 6, 6) rows 1 (3, 5, 7) more times. Piece should measure approximately 5.25 (5.25, 5, 5) in (13.5 [13.5, 12.5, 12.5] cm) from cast on edge.

Shape Shoulder:
Row 1 (RS): K1, ssk, knit to last 3 sts, k2tog, k1.
Row 2 (WS): Purl all stitches.

Repeat last 2 rows until 4 sts remain. Bind off loosely.

☞ Pockets

Using invisible sewing thread and smaller needles.

Pocket 1 (from left underarm point, count 6 sts in and 16 rows up):

Pick up and knit 15 sts. Knit 22 rows of stockinette stitch. Bind off all stitches loosely.

Pocket 2 (from left hand bottom corner of pocket, 1 count 4 sts out [away from shoulder] and 22 rows down):

Pick up and knit 13 sts. Work 18 rows of stockinette stitch. Bind off all stitches loosely.

Pocket 3 (from left hand bottom corner of pocket, 1 count 4 sts out and 5 rows up):

Pick up and knit 20 sts. Work 14 rows of stockinette stitch. Bind off all stitches loosely.

☞ Finish

Weave in all loose ends.

Wet block/shape all pieces, lying flat to dry.

Attach the sleeves.

Close side and shoulder seams with mattress stitch.

Set in sleeves with mattress stitch, easing in stitches where necessary to make a smooth join.

Attach side seams of pockets on front of the sweater in heart area, stretching them to match the sweater stitches, cast off on the top.

Pick up stitches on hemline to crochet the picot edge. In each stitch, *make 1 double crochet, make a chain of 3, double crochet in first stitch of chain, double crochet in next chain,* repeat within * in each stitch.

Pick up stitches on neckline to crochet the picot edge. In each stitch, *make 1 double crochet, make a chain of 3, double crochet in first stitch of chain, double crochet in next chain,* repeat within * in each stitch.

Pick up stitches on sleeve to crochet the edge. In each stitch make 1 double crochet. Repeat for 2 rows.

Pick up stitches on top of the pockets to crochet the picot edge. In each stitch, *make 1 double crochet, make a chain of 3, double crochet in first stitch of chain,* repeat within * in each stitch.

Weave in all loose ends.

Fill the pockets of your sweater with the memories that you want to keep close.

brifrischu was born in Aachen, Germany. After studying to be a librarian, she realized that while she loved research, she couldn't imagine life without making things. Learning how to knit prompted a career change. She earned a BA in Knitwear Design and Knitted Textiles at Nottingham Trent University after making a living as a self-employed knitwear accessory and jewelry designer. A short stint working for a major fashion company taught her how restrictive the cycle of trends could be, and in looking for alternative design projects, brifrischu discovered her niche in textiles and conceptual design. Her degree project, *No Place Like Home*, looked at ways that clothing could be made more appealing and easier to use by those with dementia. She continues to further her work in this area as a graduate student of Interaction Design at Nottingham Trent University where she researches the world of wearable technologies. *brifrischu.de*

Chapter Three

POETIC TEXTILES

I've always thought that the process of writing poems is much like knitting. If you hit a problem, like dropping a stitch, the root of the problem is often a few lines or rows back.

—poet Gwyneth Lewis

Weave & words

Poems are what you make when you observe life in a certain way. Alive to yourself in the world, observant of inner and outer reality, and connected to language.

—*poet Kim Addonizio,*
Ordinary Genius: A Guide for the Poet Within

People often have strong feelings about poetry. For some, it is a place of refuge, a way to look at the world with intention and new perspectives. Others grapple with poetry, finding it elusive and hard to understand. Most public schools teach only one type of poetry to children, the rhyming verse. While for some, rhyming verse can serve as a gateway, for others, this limited introduction can make it difficult to accept other forms—such as free verse, experimental poetry, epigrams, found poems, slam poetry, and conceits—later on. Whether through the delights of discovering the quirky insights of e.e. cummings to experiencing the candid verse of Sharon Olds or the beauty of a Pablo Neruda love poem—reading poetry can change your life. Writing poetry can create pleasure, inspire introspection, and generate the feeling of being understood. No matter what form of poetry you are drawn to, you will find that the success of a poem is usually marked by the poet's ability to communicate an emotional truth.

Just as the texture of a fiber can stir up strong feelings, so can the placement of carefully chosen words. The artists in this chapter have chosen to combine the materiality of textiles with the unruly nature of poetry. Powerful, illusive, or celebratory—textiles and poetry can complement each other in stitch and tension, weft and warp, weave and words.

I've applied for a grant to do more quilts about African-American poetry. There have been several African-American poet laureates, and the present poet laureate in the United States, Natasha Trethewey, is an African-American woman.

—*artist Marion Coleman*

Writing a poem can be like knitting a sweater. Each word, like a stitch on the needle, connects with what has come before it and what is to follow. Movement matters, and the placement of each stitch affects the final whole. To combine poetry and textiles is to take a leap of faith, both on the page and on the cloth.

Using Textiles to Talk about Poetry: The UK Poetry Project

In 2009, the UK Poetry Society rolled out a giant, handmade blanket containing Dylan Thomas's poem "In My Craft or Sullen Art" at the British Library in London. The blanket, designed by London-based Rachael Matthews and Louise Harris (the "modern haberdashers" of yarn store Prick Your Finger), is the collected work of more than 850 knitters and crocheters who made 12-in (30.5-cm) squares, each containing one letter of the alphabet. Even as individual squares were being stitched during September 2009, the final blanket design remained a mystery to those making it.

The impetus for the knitted blanket was simple: "Readers sometimes need reminding that poems don't drop out of the sky onto the Internet," said Judith Palmer, Director of the UK Poetry Society. "I hope people will see the work involved in the knitting and reflect on the poet's sleepless nights crafting the text."

The UK Poetry Project, knitted blanket, 2009, 43 x 28 ft (13 x 8.7 m).
Photo: Haley Madden

KNIT-ERATURE

The Poetry Project prompted a fun online game. At the website *poetrysociety.org.uk/content/knit/knitgame*, you can type your own poem and watch your words "knit" in digital images before your eyes.

Prompt

Write a Poem

Do you want to write a poem but find yourself unsure of how to begin? Try one of the following prompts:

1. Start a poem with the phrase "I remember." Or begin each line with "I remember."

2. Find a book of poetry that you admire and, within it, identify a poem that leaves you with a question. Ask this question in the form of a poem.

3. Change the scale: Pick something very tiny and write about it as if it is extremely large, or pick something gigantic and write about it as if it were miniature.

4. Personify: Give an inanimate object a voice. Write the poem from its point of view.

SLEEPING WITH POETRY:

An Interview with Kerry Larkin of Comma Workshop

Comma Workshop is an artisanal business in the Colorado Front Range area. Working with local quilters, designer and wordsmith **Kerry Larkin** brings together the traditional customs of quilting and storytelling with a distinctive twist. Each quilt that the workshop produces is one-of-a-kind, machine-stitched with a cursive typeface and displays an original story or poem written by Larkin.

Comma Workshop, *Rain Comes Down Like Arrows*, 2010, 100-percent cotton, 60 x 65 x 0.5 in (152.4 x 165.1 x 1.27 cm). Photo: David Tegart Photography

Q: How did Comma Workshop originate?

A: I started Comma Workshop in 2010 to bring a fresh perspective to the time-honored traditions of quilting and storytelling. I write poems and narratives about life, nature, and adventure. I stitch these into every quilt, combining typography with my cursive handwriting. My goal is to create functional heirlooms; timeless, sophisticated quilts that have a hint of playfulness.

For as long as I can remember, in any art that I've created, whether sculpture, collage, or textiles, I've always included words or stories. In 2008, I created an installation piece for a gallery in Philadelphia in which I stitched stories onto white silk. I really wanted to push this idea further. Since I was trained as an architect and designer, I wanted to explore the idea of textiles and words in a more practical sense. Making quilts was the logical solution—functional, yet beautiful.

The first Comma quilt was a wedding gift for some dear friends. It was all white with a thin line of printed fabric. Across the front I stitched the words "Hibernation wakes orange lights and sweet wonder..." referencing how we emerge from winter to the brightness of spring. They loved the quilt and suggested that I make more. The next day I registered Comma Workshop as an LLC [a limited liability company], and haven't stopped quilting since!

Q: Tell me about your writing.

A: I'm a minimalist at heart, so I love writing haiku. Each quilt design starts with a haiku. I take the feeling and energy from that haiku and build on it, creating the entire prose poem or narrative that fills the quilt. My narratives and prose poetry are descriptions of place, of how we move through spaces with heightened senses and awareness. I love describing places through my writing, capturing the emotions and feelings reflected there. The idea is that the visual comes first—if you look at the quilt from afar, it should be aesthetically pleasing. The secondary experience is the highlighted words. The third layer is composed of the words quilted into the background. I think quilting is a perfect medium for this. A quilt has three layers—the top and bottom fabric and a thin layer of batting in the middle. The quilted words actually hold the three layers together; they are a functional and necessary part of the quilt.

Q: How did you start writing poetry?

A: I've been writing for as long as I can remember. Right now, I'm inspired by nature and our place in it—whether in the Rocky Mountains, where Comma Workshop is located, rural Alabama, or western Pennsylvania. My intention is to write daily. That doesn't always happen! But if I'm continually writing, there will be a few phrases or snippets that I'll get attached to. At that point, I start to think about a quilt layout. I'll sketch a few patterns and layouts and then go back and write some more. It's a back-and-forth process.

Q: What is implicit in a poem that makes it quiltable?

A: I think the rhythm of prose poetry lends itself to quilting. My handwriting has few stops and starts, and there are barely spaces between words, so the meditative rhythm is perfect for quilting.

Top: Comma Workshop, *Wading towards Home*, 2012, 100-percent cotton, 60 x 65 x 0.5 in (152.4 x 165.1 x 1.27 cm). Photo: Jess O' Toole Photography

Bottom: Comma Workshop, *A Perfect Moon*, 2012, 100-percent cotton, 60 x 65 x 0.5 in (152.4 x 165.1 x 1.27 cm). Photo: Jess O' Toole Photography

Comma Workshop, *Aspens Whisper for More Time*, 2010, 100 percent cotton, 60 x 65 x 0.5 in (152.4 x 165.1 x 1.27 cm). Photo: David Tegart Photography

Q: Do you think that replicating the poem on a textile changes its meaning?

A: Definitely. When I write something on paper, spaces, pauses, and punctuation marks are all key parts of the piece. Yet when I quilt it, I take all of those things away. There are no longer breaks and pauses. To me, this takes the preciousness of the piece away—which is good. Just as traditional quilts have patches and patterns of color and printed fabric, the words on my quilts become those "patches."

Q: How do you choose how the poem should be rendered? And what sort of sewing techniques do you apply?

A: Writing that is long and fluid lends itself to being the cursive background of the quilts. Occasionally, I feel a strong connection to a certain phrase, for example, "Tonight, the ponderosa pines dictate our travel plans." I never know if other people will have the same affinity for a phrase like that, but for me, that phrase needs to stand out. I keep my palette of typefaces small and simple—mostly Helvetica or Times New Roman. I want my quilts to be modern yet timeless.

The cursive quilting is made with a free-motion quilting foot on a hand-guided long-arm machine. No two letters are alike. The typefaces are made with a computerized machine. After growing up doing hand-quilting, I was hesitant to use a machine, but the precise quality of the typeface juxtaposed with my own cursive handwriting creates a perfect balance in the quilts.

Comma Workshop, *Striped Dogs Howl*, 2011, 100-percent cotton, 60 x 65 x 0.5 in (152.4 x 165.1 x 1.27 cm). Photo: Ralph E. Burns Photography

Q: Your quilts contain thousands of words. How do you choose what to highlight?

A: I'm drawn to concise, descriptive phrases about place and nature. Right now, the world is over-saturated with inspirational quotes on Facebook, etc. So I choose to highlight phrases like "Space and winter wait for no one" or "Aspens whisper for more time." These phrases invite the reader into the story. ✳

PUBLIC INTERVENTIONS WITH POETRY BOMBING:

An Interview with Agustina Woodgate

In 2011, a video of a young woman identified as the "Poetry Bomber" went viral on YouTube. The short clip from a local newspaper's website captured a guerrilla artist sneaking into thrift stores in Miami, Florida, where she covertly sewed tiny labels with poems by Sylvia Plath and Li Po into the lining of garments. Originally from Buenos Aires, Agustina Woodgate is a Florida-based multi-media artist who strives to create art that encourages exchanges between people. The Poetry Bombing project was her first foray into working with textiles. *agustinawoodgate.com*

Agustina Woodgate. Poetry bombing, Miami, Florida, 2011.
Photos: Courtesy of Agustina Woodgate and Spinello Projects

Q: What inspired your poetry bombing project?

A: April is National Poetry Month in the United States [and Canada]. A colleague in Miami, Scott Cunningham, was organizing a poetry festival. His goal was to reach all the citizens he could in Miami Dade County with a poem, which I thought was incredibly ambitious. I am a big reader, but I just never end up with a book of poetry in my hands; I don't find it accessible in that way. But I contacted Scott and told him, "I'd like to help you out. Let's go for coffee." As we were talking and getting acquainted with each other, I offered my help with administrative and outreach duties. Instead, he invited me to participate in the festival. "But I'm not a poet!" I responded. What was particularly interesting to me, though, was that he was going for a broad audience. He had ambitious ideas about taking poetry outside of the poetry circuit, which I find quite hermetic. He was contacting restaurants and putting poems in the menus; he was even creating fake parking tickets with poems on them.

We went back to my studio that day. At the time, I was working on a collection of rugs made out of discarded stuffed animals. As a practice, I save everything and had saved all of the labels from them. I showed him all these jars and jars of teddy bear labels. We [decided that we] would print short poems on blank clothing labels and distribute them widely by covertly sewing them onto thrift store garments.

After that, I carried the labels with me, and I would bomb my friends' closets. "Oh, you're going to take a shower? Sure, go ahead!" The last time that I was in a plane, I sewed one on my seat. I figured that I could really do this everywhere!

Q: Thrifted garments seem to be connected to history. Is this why you chose to do this project at thrift stores?

A: My entire practice is created from objects that are already in circulation. This is intentional. I use objects because of their meanings. If you find that there's a poem in your clothes, it's as if the garment is carrying a story. People perceived the poems as messages. They'd buy them because they were carrying a message, a sign, some kind of premonition! This idea shifts the impact of the poem itself, as if the clothes are telling you something, which is part of the absurdity of this project.

When I started poetry bombing, I began in secret, because I thought, why get permission? I might as well just start doing it. I got kicked out of three stores, but then I also met a cashier who could not believe that I was doing it for free, who told me, "This is amazing. You should get paid!" I learned how to sneak into stores. I would arrive with pre-threaded needles in my coat. The whole thing was so absurd! You'll suspect that someone is stealing something, sure, but not sewing.

Q: How did you choose the items of clothing that you were going to sew poems into?

A: I didn't. The idea was to be really quick. I selected garments that were in the hidden corners of the stores. I had no plan as to where I was going to sew the tags. At first, I sewed them in the label area, then I realized other possibilities and that's when it started to get funny. On a pair of pants, I'd sew the label in the pocket or inside the pants so that the wearer might find it when getting undressed. I started thinking about the element of surprise.

Top: Agustina Woodgate sewing poetry tags at a Miami thrift store, 2011. Photo: Jacob Katel, *Miami New Times*

Bottom: Agustina Woodgate. Poetry bombing, Miami, Florida, 2011. Photos: Courtesy of Agustina Woodgate and Spinello Projects

I'm really into the idea of the gift economy. What happened with this project was interesting because I experienced the effectiveness of a gift. The poems didn't have my name attached to them, just the name of the poet. But because I was part of the poetry festival, someone from the local newspaper called me to document this action. A really cool guy came over from the paper who totally understood the guerrilla aspect of the project and hid his camera while filming. He made a video and posted it on the newspaper site with my name. I didn't know what sort of impact the video would have, but it went viral within a month. It ended up in *The Guardian*, *Time*, and *Huffington Post*. In three months it had over 100,000 hits. I started to receive emails from people all over the world, thanking me. The process was very fluid, and its intention was purely to spread a gift. I was experiencing the effects of a sincere gesture.

Q: Do you think your relationship with the person reading the poem is a personal one? Or is it a public experience?

A: There a merger between public art and personal experience, because it is public art, but the encounter is so personal. It's not a poem on a billboard, which is truly in the public sphere. It's not everyone seeing the same poem at the same time. I'm using the public realm in an intimate way, a one-on-one encounter. The moment when the person finds the poem is perceived as a sign—they feel it's special, it's like reading a fortune cookie.

Q: You have a very different project, in which you make rugs out of stuffed animals. How did that idea come to you?

A: I returned to the idea of what an object carries after having been owned. Perhaps every single one of us has owned a stuffed animal and given it name, and although the thing is not alive, we make it alive with our imaginations. Again, I'm exploring the absurdity of our relationship with objects. This idea transcends borders. It is about an archetype, a pattern of human behavior.

These rugs are created out of used, discarded stuffed animals. I'm removing the skins of these animal to construct rugs. Most people have feelings attached to these objects, and some people can't get rid of their old stuffed animals because they are too meaningful, and they carry too many memories. At the same time, they are not used anymore, they are just collecting dust on shelves or in closets. The moment that I opened the first bear and realized it was just like an animal skin, it all started to make some sense. I use stuffed animals not necessarily recycle materials, but to recycle meaning, memories, and this collective understanding of bonding. After you let them go, they become abandoned. No one wants a used stuffed animal. They want the one that they had. ✳

Agustina Woodgate, *No Rain, No Rainbows*, 2011, stuffed animal skins,
16 x 9.5 ft (4.8 x 2.89 m). Photo: Anthony Spinello

Project

Wear Your Words: A Poetry Scarf

LEANNE PRAIN

Our lives need more poetry! Make your favorite poems into wearable items by writing on cloth. With common household bleach, you can create a poetry scarf, marking a beloved poem onto soft jersey. As when you begin to write a poem, you won't know what this project will look like until it's finished; the final result depends on how the base fabric was dyed. Your bleached words may end up pure white, or they may take on some of the properties of the existing dye. Wear your own words or pick a quote from your favorite poet and you can take poetry with you anywhere that you go.

(This project is not limited to poetry—a micro-story, a few lines of dialogue, or a manifesto would also fit well on a scarf of this size. But you don't have to make a scarf, either. Write an ode to the night sky on a bed sheet or make a found poem from an old grocery list and write it on a tote bag.)

CAUTION: Bleach is a toxic substance and should be kept out of the reach of children and pets. Wear gloves while using, and protect your clothes and eyes.

- 100 percent cotton jersey knit in black or another dark color, cut to measure 21 x 70 in (53.34 cm x 1.78 m), pre-washed and pressed flat

- 2–3 swatches of scarf fabric for test-dyeing, each measuring 4 x 4 in (10.16 x 10.16 cm)

- 1 20 x 20 in (50.8 x 50.8 cm) cardboard (optional)

- a covered and protected work-surface
  TIP: wrap a sheet of plastic around your table.

- fabric scissors

- 2 cups (500 mL) undiluted, fabric-safe bleach

- 1 empty Jacquard syringe needle tip or Fineline applicator tool with a fine tip (available at most art stores). In a pinch, a small synthetic-bristled paint brush can be used instead.

- dressmaker's chalk pencil (optional)

- ruler (optional)

- sewing needle

- matching thread (optional: to finish raw edges of scarf)

- rags

- plastic gloves

- ceramic or glass bowl

- fabric weights (rocks, paperweights, or other heavy household items) or bulldog clips

- a poem. This project uses "Day" by Laura Farina (see p. 74). Use Laura's poem or write one of your own.

  Note: Consider whether your project will be made public online or will ever be for sale. You will need permission to use another person's text in your own works. Reproducing someone else's work without their permission is not only inconsiderate, it's against the law.

SKILLS

handwriting

basic sewing skills (optional)

Day

9 a.m.
Junk mail recycled.
Slippers stepped out of
and doors locked behind.

11:30 a.m.
The clank of the mailbox closing
is from another time.

Noon
How sunlight touches sidewalk
is a private matter
between sunlight and the sidewalk.

2 p.m.
Brown things
step aside
for green things.

4:45 p.m.
Winds have already parted
all the hair
they can part for one day.

5.30 p.m.
Interview
with a lonely
piece of highway.

9 p.m.
This window
might open.
This sky
might spill
and pool.

Laura Farina's first book of poetry, *This Woman Alphabetical*, won the Archibald Lampman Award. Originally from Ottawa, she now lives in Vancouver.

☛ What Does Your Poem Look Like?

Before you begin, read the poem and think about what sort of handwriting would best express its meaning. Should it be all lowercase? Should the lines run diagonally across the fabric? Could it be written backwards? Has the poet chosen certain lines for emphasis? Practice drawing out the design a few times on a piece of paper.

☛ Create a Swatch Test

Try a bleach test on a few swatches of fabric before dyeing the scarf. As your fabric will already contain dye of an unknown origin, the results of bleaching your words will be slightly unpredictable, but definitely interesting!

1. Carefully fill applicator or syringe with bleach (do this over a sink). Make sure that a cap blocks the writing tip so that you don't spill the bleach.

2. Place three test swatches side by side. Practice making a few lines on the fabric to test the thickness of the writing implement. If syringe is too fine, try using a small synthetic-bristled paintbrush.

3. Label the swatches: half-hour, one hour, and two hours. Place them in a dry, warm place (preferably in the sun) for time denoted. You can set a kitchen timer to remind you when to check each one.

4. Wearing gloves, rinse each swatch out in cold water at the specified time and compare results.

5. Depending on the dye that was used in the piece of fabric you've chosen, the writing could look red, orange, pink, yellow, or white. Which effect do you like best? That's the time allotment to use to bleach the scarf. If they all look similar, choose the swatch with the minimum drying time so the bleach does less damage to the fiber.

Brown things

step aside

for green f

1-45 p

winds

MAKE THE SCARF

1. While swatches are drying, place scarf fabric right-side up onto cardboard so that it is completely flat and taut but not stretched. Weigh corners down or use bulldog clips to secure fabric to cardboard.

2. Use dressmaker's chalk to sketch design onto fabric, making sure that poem fits on scarf. For even lines, use ruler as a guide for baseline of text. Keep fabric as flat as possible, but handle lightly to avoid wrinkling it. If fabric becomes wrinkled, smooth it out. Sketch out letterforms. The chalk will fade out in the washing stage, so don't worry about making a mistake. The goal is to create a guideline for the bleach.

3. Use a steady hand to draw with applicator, brush, or syringe and trace the chalk markings. Move slowly but don't hold your hand in one place too long or bleach will flood the area and the line will appear thicker. The bleach will start to transform the fabric right away, revealing your words as you write.

4. Once you've covered the entire design, wait a few minutes. Check to see if there are any uncovered areas that need a touch-up.

5. Let the piece sit untouched for the amount of time determined by your swatch test.

6. Wearing gloves, rinse scarf well with cold water, then hand wash it in soap and water and hang to dry.

You now have a permanent poem that you can wear around your neck whenever you feel poetic.

Chapter Four

TEXTILES OF PROTEST, POLITICS, AND POWER

Cloth can be the drawing board, the visual shout of injustice. Cloth should not be overly romanticized as only having sweet statements of "the world as it is."

—**Andrea M. Heckman,** *Woven Stories: Andean Textiles and Rituals*

Human experience

People associate embroidery with women [who have] too much time on their hands. We need to show how historically important it is. The Bayeux Tapestry ... is 1,000 years old. It contains scenes that [could be right out of today's] news, [scenes depicting] the butchery of war. It is a miracle that the tapestry survived. Textiles are living history.

—*Bettina Matzkuhn*

While most people are drawn to stories with happy outcomes, sorrow and injustice are part of the human experience. Politics and protest are therefore an inherent part of life, and textiles have long been part of these traditions. Fabric has served as a tool of political communication throughout history, and at times it has been as a medium of communication in places where it was illegal, or even deadly, to speak or write. Textiles can be used as a subversive way to tell stories because fiber arts may appear powerless to the unobservant. This chapter explores textiles as powerful tools that can make a suppressed story heard.

Even in societies where free speech is encouraged, textiles provide a space for people to express strong emotions, memories, and opinions. Whether through yarn bombing, *arpilleras*, protest banners, armbands, stitched manifestos, craftivism, or subverting the politics of stitching itself, textiles can allow us to speak and tell our different truths.

Rugs of Resistance

Afghanistan has a long history of creating pictorial rugs. Known for pile-woven carpets filled with symbols of life and faith, weavers of traditional Afghan rugs have adjusted their designs to incorporate images of war and destruction. These Afghan "war rugs" function as a news report, spanning the period of the Soviet invasion of 1979 to the Taliban rule and the American occupation.

Many of the war rugs are attributed to the Baluch (a.k.a. Baluchi or Beluchi), a nomadic group of weavers who occupy the Afghan-Iranian-Pakistani borders. The carpets are generally dark red, brown, and dark blue, and the warp is made from wool or goat hair. Their design is geometric, and where such rugs traditionally showed flowers, birds, vases, and animals, newer motifs include army tanks, machine guns, and helicopters.

Afghan War Rugs in Bazaar Kabul, Afghanistan, 2011. Photos: Ron Jobo

Following the attacks on the US in September of 2001, the influx of military personnel, aid workers, diplomats, and journalists into Afghanistan created a market for such rugs. Demand for them has meant that they are increasingly created in workshop settings and made to be sold. The military imagery on the rugs has shifted too; stylized imagery of Soviet war equipment has given way to hyper-realistic renditions of American tanks and aircraft.

As Afghan rug-making moves from the work of individual weavers to workshops and factories, there is debate about the validity of the rugs as a tool for resistance. While some experts suggest that the weavers are catering only to their North American collectors, others, such as curator Michele Hardy, have suggested that the rugs offer a venue for expression in a society that has little space for discourse amid media and cultural propaganda. In response to an exhibit of war rugs she co-curated with Robert Fyke at the Nickle Arts Museum at the University of Calgary in 2006, she wrote: "Weavers of war rugs are actively recovering, even reinventing, Afghan history, critiquing the war and Western stereotypes. War rugs express their creative engagement with color and design, as well as war, political, and economic change."

AUTHOR CHARLES DICKENS

knew the connection between stitching and making a revolution. In *A Tale of Two Cities*, his character Madame Defarge, who secretly works for the French Revolution, includes the names of people who are about to be executed by guillotine in her knitting.

Spinning for Freedom

During the 1920s, Mahatma Gandhi believed that India could be freed from British rule and achieve self-governance through economic independence gained, in part, via local cloth production. Cotton pickers in India made a mere seven cents per day. The raw cotton was placed on British ships and sent to the UK where it was spun by laborers who made significantly more. The bolts of cloth were returned to India where they were sold to the upper classes, who were profiting from the work of the underpaid cotton pickers. Gandhi proposed that if Indians spun their own cotton to make *khadi* (cloth), the country could become self-sufficient. Gandhi himself spun yarn, and he would only wear robes made from cotton that he spun.

In 1946, *LIFE* magazine photographer Margaret Bourke-White captured Gandhi at his spinning wheel. The importance of the spinning wheel to him is evident in the reporter's notes that she sent back to the *LIFE* magazine office with the photographs: "[Gandhi] spins every day for 1 hr. beginning usually at 4. All members of his ashram must spin. He and his followers encourage everyone to spin...Spinning is raised to the heights almost of a religion with Gandhi and his followers. The spinning wheel is sort of an Ikon [sic] to them. Spinning is a cure all, and is spoken of in terms of the highest poetry."

Telling Stories under Dictatorship: The Chilean *Arpillera*

In the 1970s and '80s, Chilean *arpilleras* (the word means burlap in Spanish) helped communicate the stories of a silenced people. The *arpilleras*, small, three-dimensional pictures made of fabric, depicted the state of the country under military oppression, with images of police brutality, kidnappings, and poverty. Chilean woman sewing together in workshops commonly created these works, which often only measured about twelve-in (30.48-cm) square. Remarkably, these powerful images were created under a violent dictatorship. In 1973, Chile came under the domination of General Pinochet through a bloody military coup. For the next fifteen years, Chileans who spoke out against the regime were killed, tortured, imprisoned, and "disappeared" by the thousands. Men were dragged from their homes by military police during the night, never to be heard from again. Families could not learn the whereabouts of their loved ones, the detained or disappeared, whose fates remained a mystery. The military did not provide any explanations to the widows of these disappeared men beyond suggesting that their husbands had left them. In this patriarchal society, women were kept to traditional roles as homemakers and were financially dependent on the men, in whose absence families often became impoverished.

The Vicariate of Solidarity, a human-rights organization under the auspices of the Roman Catholic Church in Santiago, hosted what became the first *arpillera* workshop in 1974. Many destitute women had turned to the church for comfort, and the church offered the women a sewing workshop that encouraged them to express their creativity while earning an income. The church provided them with cloth, thread, and needles with which the women could create colorful pictures sewn on burlap that would be sold outside of Chile. Revenue from these sales would provide living expenses for the women.

Marjorie Agosin, herself a Chilean exile, spent twenty years interviewing *arpilleristas*, the women who made *arpilleras*, for her book *Tapestries of Hope, Threads of Love: The Arpillera Movement in Chile 1974–1994*. She wrote, "I visited the workshops in Santiago and asked the women why they make *arpilleras* with such tenacity. The voices mingled in their eagerness to share their story. 'We are here to denounce what happened to us and to put our anguish into the *arpilleras* so others will know.'"

Arpilleras are commonly constructed with layers of fabric held together with a blanket stitch. These small images are created with appliquéd cotton, burlap, or synthetic fiber. The pieces are often embellished with embroidery wool and other materials, such as human hair or clay. Background fabrics show rural or urban landscapes, often with hints of blue sky or outlines of the Andes Mountains. The backs of the pieces are almost always lined with heavy burlap.

In a society in which women were not encouraged to speak up or assert their politics, the *arpilleras* served as a platform for the crafters to express their anger, sadness, and suffering.

These women makers took risks—and learned to take advantage of the fact that their existence was ignored by the dictatorship. Traditional designs evolved as the women began to adorn the pieces with slogans such as "No More Torture," and "Where Are They?" As the church exported the *arpilleras* for sale, the story of what was happening in Chile began to spread beyond its borders. While a man might be disappeared for attending a political protest, a woman could ask pointed questions through her sewing and go undetected. On average, the woman making the *arpilleras* created four per month, and hundreds were shipped outside of Chile. The organizational power of the *arpilleras* did not end with the sewing workshops. Emboldened by their sewing circles, some women began to organize protest marches and wore photos of their disappeared loved ones on their chests.

When Pinochet was finally removed from power in 1990, the women of Chile did not stop making *arpilleras*. The subject matter has changed over time, encompassing parts of current life under democratic governance. Sometimes happy, sometimes sad, the *arpilleras* continue to reflect the day-to-day experiences of women in South America. They have since been adopted as a form of art by the woman of Peru where they are called *cuadros* (pictures) and have taken on their own cultural lens in the Peruvian context.

ImBLEACHment AND PUBLIC SATIRE:

An Interview with Diane Bush

Diane Bush lives in Las Vegas and calls herself an "unapologetic arts activist" whose life and art have been shaped by the Vietnam War and the peace movement. When still a pre-teen living in a liberal Jewish family in Buffalo, New York, her older brother encouraged her to read Karl Marx, Chairman Mao, Vance Packard, J.D. Salinger, and Aldous Huxley. At an early age, she began painting anti-war protest signs with local radicals. At eighteen, she married a draft dodger and moved from the US to the UK, where she devoted herself to learning photography. She was influenced by the work of Lewis Hine, who used his camera as a tool for social reform. After returning to the US and earning an MFA in photography, Diane worked as a staff photographer for ABC and PBS television stations, ran a photo department for a private liberal college, and since 1999, has worked as a public servant for Clark County in Las Vegas as a curator, grant writer, educator, publicist, and museum advocate. Currently, she is enjoying her best assignment yet—supervising an active seniors' center with an enthusiastic yarn bombing group called the West Flamingo Yarnstormers. *dianebush.net*

Left: Gulf War vet, Al, with his blanket, in Las Vegas, 2011. Photo: Las Vegas Occupy; Right: Tamara and friends with her ImBLEACHment blanket in Las Vegas, 2011. Photo: Diane Bush

Q: Can you tell me about your work and your ImBLEACHment projects?

A: I use bleach and photography in my work. The images that I create are transferred to woven blankets that are sometimes worn as ponchos. I specialize in political satire. My first was a public participation performance piece just before the election of Barack Obama in 2008 called The ImBLEACHment of George W. Bush. I invited the public to help me bleach out a large photo of Bush by throwing small vials of diluted bleach on the photo. I was so pleased with the result that I wanted to continue with the technique. The act of watching the emulsion melt away reminded me of stories I'd heard on National Public Radio about jealous suitors or husbands in India and Pakistan who threw bleach in the faces of girls and women in acts of horrendous misogyny. This idea led me to using fabrics, and it inspired me to return to performance art.

Q: Can you tell me about *The Big Cover-Up*, which involved the use of textiles?

A: I transferred bleached photos to woven blankets by enlisting the assistance of weavers. I then gave the blankets away to Occupiers and the homeless in several [US] cities. After the first ImBLEACHments, I wanted to continue doing political satire. I had participated in a few more public art events where I invited people to help me bleach photos of corrupt politicians who cheated on wives, got involved in shady deals, etc. These events provided me with a lot of photo fodder to use at a later date. Then I was offered an opportunity to curate an exhibit at the Marjorie Barrick Museum at University of Nevada, Las Vegas.

I was tired of spending over $1,000 for framing each exhibit, so I had the idea to use fabric instead of photo paper. My first thought was to digitally print photos on fabric to create a quilt of some kind, but my husband pointed out that a quilt would be too complicated and suggested using a woven blanket like one that he had seen at a drugstore photo counter. The prototype for the first one was called *Blanket of Lies*, and it contained a photo of a much-reviled political candidate who had been ImBLEACHed at one of the performances. I emailed the photo to some weavers in Kentucky, who charged me $75. It was a gamble, but the end result was far more luxurious and colorful than I had hoped for. It hung at the exhibit, and later I made a poncho out of it. At the same time, the Occupy movement was in the news, and I had been looking for a way to help Iraqi War vets, so giving away blankets to the Occupiers seemed to be the perfect solution. USA Projects, which had asked me to produce a video for a crowd-funding project, partially funded the distribution of blankets to occupiers in Los Angeles, Buffalo, and Las Vegas.

Q: Does *The Big Cover-Up* tell a story or conceal one?

A: This project's story is three-fold: It's about an artist, her family, her influences, and her desire to make the world a bit better, in the spirit of those early "concerned photographers," whom we would now call "activist artists." It's about how her art matured from simple journalism to performance art, alternative processes, and materials.

It's also a message to other artists: Don't be afraid to say what is on your mind. You can safely say pretty much anything, if you use humor. In the US, parody and satire are essentially protected by law. *The Big Cover-Up* pays homage to the Yippie pranksters of the late sixties who were inspired by Abbie Hoffman's book *Steal This Book* and the use of absurdity and humor in art.

But most of all, it's the story of those left out in the cold, both figuratively and literally: it's the story of a couple that lives under a bridge; a woman who loses a job due to sexual harassment and can't find another; a young student who had to drop out of college because he could not afford it; a homeless Vietnam vet who never received treatment for PTSD; a blue-collar worker in his sixties with no job prospects—it's really their stories. ✴

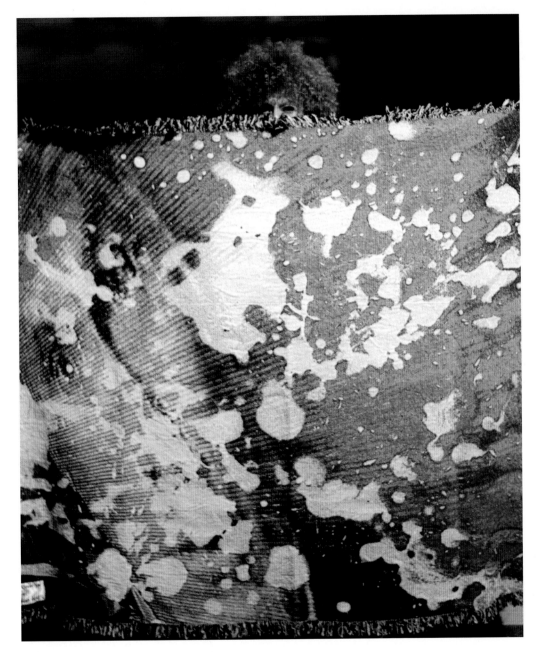

Diane Bush, *Mitt Romney ImBLEACHed*, digital print, 2012, 8 x 10 in (20.32 x 25.4 cm). Photo: Diane Bush

Prompt

Make Your Voice Heard

Want to try your hand at creating textiles of protest?
Try one of the following experiments:

- Subvert the politics of stitching by placing handicrafts where they "don't belong." Create some cozy graffiti with knitting, crochet, felting, or weaving (a.k.a. yarn bombing) to bring attention to something that others should be aware of, whether an overlooked statue of a forgotten hero or a community center that is doing great work.

- Protest banners can be painted, dyed, woven, or stitched. Use the medium of your choice to get across your opinion on environmental, social, or political issues.

- Get people talking through craft. Pick a worthy topic of discussion and invite a sewing circle of quilters, embroiderers, knitters, or weavers to stitch 'n' bitch as a way to find and share solutions for your cause.

- Write a short manifesto on how you'd like to change the world. Take the time to commit it to a time-intensive craft, such as cross-stitch, and add it to a pillowcase or a wall hanging. The time it takes to stitch the piece will allow you to meditate on how to put your thoughts into action.

TELLING COMMUNITY STORIES THROUGH
S.T.I.T.C.H.E.D:
An Interview with Climbing PoeTree

Alixa Garcia and **Naima Penniman** make up the dynamic spoken word, multi-media performance duo called Climbing Poetree. They've performed together for more than ten years; their powerful live touring show is dedicated to sharing stories, building community, and working toward social justice. Since their first national tour in 2003, they've worked on a project called *S.T.I.T.C.H.E.D.* They distribute six-inch (15.24-cm) fabric squares and Sharpies to their audience members, whom they invite to share a personal story. Through *S.T.I.T.C.H.E.D*, they have collected a nation's worth of stories—personal, dark, inspiring, or aspirational. Each square is stitched into a colorful banner that is strung up and shared through their performances and educational workshops. As self-described "agents of change," Alixa and Naima strive to strengthen the voices of the unheard and underrepresented, one stitch at a time. *climbingpoetree.com*

Climbing PoeTree, Tenth Anniversary Celebration at the National Black Theatre in Harlem, NY, July 27, 2013. Photo: Jessica Ho

Q: Who is Climbing PoeTree?

A: Naima: We are performance poets, cultural activists, and multi-media artists. We are based in Brooklyn, New York, and have been collaborating for ten years. We are guided by our vision for social justice and healing. Our motto is that our art is our weapon, our medicine, our voice, and our vision. We are really intentional about the poetry we write, the theater that we create, the murals that we paint. We broadcast stories from the communities we represent—which often go unheard or missing in mainstream media—using them as a tool for raising consciousness. We see stories as a way of healing from injustice and trauma, a way to break down barriers between us to promote justice. We see ourselves as mediators between community and cultures so we can recognize the oneness that we need—and not just talk about our struggles, but how much our liberation is dependent upon and interconnected with each other's peace, justice, and healing.

Alixa: We met through [Naima's] mom ten years ago. I'm from Colombia originally, and when we first met, I was doing work around the fumigations that the United States did in Colombia to eradicate coca and poppy plants. The fumigations poisoned a large section of the country, killing small children and making adults seriously ill. The cancer rates [in Columbia] are ridiculous, and the land is poisoned. I was looking at the international face of the war on drugs and how it affects my country. Naima, meanwhile, was in upstate New York working with incarcerated women, teaching them how to write poetry. Most of these women were incarcerated for non-violent drug offences.

Climbing PoeTree, Tenth Anniversary Celebration at the National Black Theatre in Harlem, NY, July 27, 2013. Photo: Jessica Ho

We were both poets and decided to put together a theater-poetry production that looked at these two faces of the war on drugs. We created a multi-media piece that was all in rhyme. In the performance, our story lines are parallel: Naima represented a mother who lost her child to the prison system, and I was a mother who lost her child to the fumigations. Whenever those stories intersected, we would speak at the same time, and this is where our multi-voice duo originated.

Naima: The show brought to us the power of our art in a very tangible way. We got to see how we could start dialogue and catalyze action around these issues that we are so passionate about. We saw that happen in cities around the US when we toured the show. Since that time, we aim to sustain the momentum that has been building since the beginning.

Q: How did *S.T.I.T.C.H.E.D* come about?

A: Naima: As poets, we recognize the importance of storytelling. We challenged ourselves to think of ways to facilitate and capture the cross-pollination of community stories we heard while on tour. We have the immense privilege of meeting so many incredible people. Rather than be a mouthpiece for their stories, we wondered how we could direct others' voices, to allow others to speak their own truths. While we were getting ready for a big national tour called Migration, we came up with the idea of collecting people's stories on pieces of fabric and then sewing them together. We ended up calling it *S.T.I.T.C.H.E.D*, which stands for Stories, Testimonies, Intentions, Truths, Confessions, Healing, Expression, and Dreams.

We placed pieces of fabric on the audience's chairs and gave them the opportunity to write something after the show was finished—a story that they wanted to testify to, something they lived, or inspiring advice that they wanted to give to the world. The fabric squares, sewn together, have become an incredible way for us to transform space. We have collected thousands of stories. We can drape huge rooms, enormous performance spaces surrounding the audience, with them. They transform workshop spaces, too. A lot of the institutions where we work are in need of that—high schools, universities, prisons. There's nothing like all that color and language to transform a space and create the healing environment we desire.

Alixa: The project launched when Hurricane Katrina hit in 2005. The week before we left to go on tour, we saw a map in the newspaper that showed where all of the Katrina survivors had ended up. It happened to be all of the cities we were going to. A lot of the first fabric squares were made by people who had been evacuated. It was universally poetic, given the direction our work was headed in.

Q: It sounds like *S.T.I.T.C.H.E.D* has become a living history project.

A: Naima: We encouraged people to date their fabric squares because we feel that they are living history. The history books often get written by the victors, not the captives. We needed to uplift the voices of everyday folks in the world, not just those invested in maintaining the status quo. Whose voices don't get a platform? How can we bear witness to each other? All of these voices form a tapestry in a symbolic

and yet very real way. It is a folk media project. Reclaiming our own history and stories gives us the power to direct and sculpt and write the stories that we are walking through.

Q: Do you find any patterns in the stories that people share with you?

A: Alixa: One of the patterns that stands out in every show is that of sexual assault and abuse. There is also the story of incarceration, whether that of the person writing or someone in their family. Trauma affects not only the victim, but also the perpetrator. We try to find compassion for both, because only those who are most hurt themselves hurt others. There is as much trauma in being an oppressor as there is in being oppressed. I feel that because the project is anonymous, it allows people to speak a truth that they wouldn't normally dare to. They can write it down; it becomes a first step toward healing.

Naima: We've also had a number of coming-out stories or people announcing their plans to come out in future. One fabric square that I loved read, "I'm out of the closet in 2008." I like to think about what their experience must have been like. I appreciate that a lot of people use *S.T.I.T.C.H.E.D* as a place for casting intentions and making commitments.

The performance that Alixa and I do is about stepping into our power, being agents of change, not just on a personal but a societal level. It is a rallying cry to take charge of the times in which we live, to make real change.

Alixa: I love that people just cheer each other on: "I'm here with you. I see you," or "You are my brother, you are my sister." A lot of them write to complete strangers: "I

Climbing PoeTree, Tenth Anniversary Celebration at the National Black Theatre in Harlem, NY, July 27, 2013. Photos: Jessica Ho

recognize you. I see you." That's the power that comes with *S.T.I.T.C.H.E.D.* You can read something completely tragic and you can relate to it, or you can be amazed by that person's survival. You can hear the encouragement that you have been needing, or you can see someone being courageous enough to say what you haven't been able to say—yet.

Q: There must be a great sense of responsibility that you feel regarding how these stories come together. How do you decide on this?

A: Naima: Most often, before sewing them, we arrange the squares by size so they fit together in strips with alternating colors. We love that it represents our society, all of these different voices coming together. There is often a divine guidance in the workshops; often the first fabric square that you read is the one that you relate to the most. You gravitate toward the one that could have been your own journal entry that morning, the one that's an answer to a prayer.

Q: Could *S.T.I.T.C.H.E.D* be the new American flag?

A: Alixa: Even though it is portable, it is very heavy. We travel with fifty lbs (22.68 kg) of it, but that is only one quarter of the entire project. We joke that it is the prototype for a new American flag, as the red, white, and blue doesn't represent a lot of people in the nation, particularly in the last decade, since 9/11. People have a new consciousness about what is happening. [This is an] enormous tapestry of colors and handwriting, languages and drawings. It feels like an authentic flag that represents the nation: it's 99.9-percent US voices—immigrant, non-immigrant, living on reservations and in prisons, elementary school children—every facet of society. That, to me, is a flag.

Naima: We joke that this is our suggestion for a more appropriate banner. We say, imagine a time when *S.T.I.T.C.H.E.D* is big enough to wrap around the entire White House.

Alixa: My most moving moment with *S.T.I.T.C.H.E.D* was in a juvenile detention center in Iowa, where we were working with young women. As we were putting it up all around the room, the guards were looking at us like there must be a rule against this somewhere. The young women who came in had a tough exterior and were ready to act out in some kind of way, but they were met with all this color and softness. By the end of the first workshop, the oldest and longest-incarcerated woman was crying and saying that she'd never felt so free; she could write her own story, go deep within herself and pull out images and poetry and create a place to be the artist that she is. To hear someone who has been in jail for so long say that was really powerful. That's the power of the art. Even if we wrote a million poems, it would not be as potent as letting people speak in their own voices. ✳

Alixa Garcia and Naima Penniman of Climbing PoeTree, 2012. Photo: Pablo Aguilar

Project

Resistance Mask

SARAH CORBETT

Sarah Corbett's approach to craftivism is to expose the scandal of global poverty and human rights injustices through the power of craft and public art and to encourage people to do something about these issues. She believes this demonstrates a valid form of activism, with both a personal and political impact. As a type of "slow activism," her projects are as much about changing an individual's attitudes and behaviors as they are about challenging the structures of injustice. "The pieces are hung in relevant public spaces to provoke thought and discussion. By making the pieces small and beautiful, I hope that people choose to engage with the message rather than feel it is forced upon them. This results in deeper and more long-lasting engagement. These masks can be very striking, raising issues of oppression and censorship." Use this project to make a cross-stitched face mask about injustice, global poverty, and human rights.

Cross-stitch and backstitch are meditative crafts. The repetition helps focus the mind, taking away the noise and anxiety of the world to concentrate on the message. The mask is compact and light, so it can be done anywhere—and maybe open up discussions about with intrigued onlookers.

TIP: Use cotton fabric with a small pattern linked to the issue you wish to draw attention to: For example, use a pattern with small flowers if the message is about protecting the environment or a print of happy people if writing about equality.

TOOLS & MATERIALS

- 4.33 x 2.76 in (11 x 7 cm) white 14-count Aida cloth

- fabric for mask: 5.90 x 7.87 in (15 x 20 cm) including 0.78 in (2 cm) edge light-weight cotton fabric with small pattern

- quilt wadding (batting) 5.11 x 3.54 in (13 x 9 cm) approx., 0.2 in (5 mm) thick

- size 8 embroidery needle

- blunt tapestry needle for cross-stitch

- 1 skein DMC #310 (black)

- 2–3 skeins DMC in bright, cheery colors, to suit patterned cotton

- 2 11-in (27.94-cm) lengths of 0.125-in (3-mm) round corded elastic ribbon

- buttons, sequins, ribbon, etc., for embellishments (optional)

- Craftivist Collective label
  (available at *craftivist-collective.com*)

- embroidery scissors

- fabric scissors

- cross-stitch or backstitch alphabet pattern in a font that you like. A variety of alphabets can be purchased at your local craft store or downloaded from the Internet. Be sure to choose letters that are small enough that the whole message will fit onto your mask. Letters that are 0.25 (0.63 cm) in size or smaller are recommended. Backstitch is recommended for longer statements.

- 1 sheet graph paper

- 1 Velcro strap, 1.97 in (5 cm) long, 0.2 in (0.5 cm) wide

SKILLS

basic counted cross-stitch. The use of backstitch is handy for longer messages.

basic hand sewing, mostly backstitch

CREATE YOUR PROTEST STATEMENT

Use metaphors, symbols, quotes, stories, alliterations, and rhythms so that your message stays in people's heads and keeps them thinking and talking.

Phrase your thoughts as questions. If you question injustice, prompt people to think about possible responses rather than preaching at them.

Take time to find the right place to install your piece. A mask about sweatshops could go on a shop-window manne-quin; a piece about inequality could be placed on a statue near a financial district. The statue needs to be human-sized and placed in a spot that is not too high up, so that people will be able to read the message on the mask.

Small is beautiful. Inspire, don't intimidate.

Facts and stats can get people thinking, but avoid over-whelming viewers with numbers that are just too enormous to comprehend.

Make your message positive, hopeful, and encouraging so that people want to share it with friends through social media and think about how they can be part of the change they wish to see in the world.

CROSS-STITCH THE MESSAGE

Cut 14-count Aida white cloth approximately 4.72 x 7.08 in (12 x 8 cm) (leave some excess space around your design so that the edge can be trimmed later). Plan out your design on graph paper, making stitches for each letter on paper. Make sure that you count enough squares on which to fit slogan.

Once design is planned out, cut DMC #310 (black) floss approximately 1 yd (1 m) long. Divide the strand in half, so that you have a length of three strands together. Save the remaining three strands to use later. Start your first cross-stitch by bringing your needle through from the back side of the work to the front, pushing it through at top right-hand corner of fabric. Count at least three squares from edge, push tapestry needle up through bottom left-hand corner of square, then bring it down through the top right-hand corner of square.

Repeat to form second leg of the cross: from wrong side of fabric, insert needle into top left-hand corner and complete stitch by pushing through the right side of the fabric to the bottom right-hand corner.

When you come to the end of the thread or need to switch colors, complete the cross you're stitching and weave end of thread in and out of the back of your stitches. Snip your loose threads close to the fabric.

When working with backstitch, move from right to left. Bring needle up from the back side of the fabric to the front. Make the first stitch by pushing needle into right side of fabric. Bring needle up in front of (to the left of) thread by the same distance. Keep bringing needle back to the previous stitch each time, keeping length of each stitch as consistent as possible. The shorter the stitch, the neater they will look. When patterns call for stitches of varying lengths, you can use a mixture of backstitch and cross-stitch.

👉 CONSTRUCT YOUR MASK

Press and trim embroidered Aida cloth so that it measures a maximum of 4.33 x 2.76 in (11 x 7 cm). Center embroidery on patterned cotton 0.25 in (0.64 cm) from sides, leaving at least 1.97 in (5 cm) from top.

Appliqué embroidery onto cotton fabric using running stitch.

You can also add embellishments (buttons, sequins) in the shape of symbols that fit the message and a Craftivist Collective label.

Wrap the patterned cotton fabric around batting with the right side of the fabric facing out. Tuck the raw edges of the fabric under so that the mask measures no more than 5.11 x 3.54 in (13 x 9 cm).

Flipping the piece over, tuck all raw edges under and, using an iron, press raw edges of fabric back to make a clean edge. Stitch pieces of fabric together over the wadding using a backstitch so the fabric forms a tube, then fold and stitch down the ends.

Now you are ready to fasten the elastics that will hold the mask to the face. Each elastic is designed to loop around an ear. To start, pin both corded elastic ribbons onto back of mask at each side. Create two loops with your lengths of cord, and place one on each side of the back of the mask, so that the raw ends face toward the center of the mask, approximately 0.5 in (1.25 cm) from the side. Pin the loops into place. Each loop should have a span of about 5 in (12.7 cm) so that the mask can be held in place with your ears. After testing the placement, stitch the loops into place with a needle and thread.

👉 PUT THE MASK ON

When you've chosen a statue or mannequin for the mask, attach it using the straps at the back, hooking the elastic loops together firmly. It is best to be stealth about these things—check over your shoulder and make sure no one sees your installation in progress!

Take a high resolution photograph to share online. Write a blog about the mask and send it to *craftivist.collective@gmail.com.*

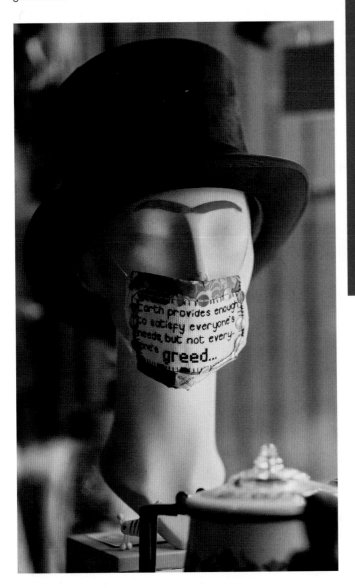

Sarah Corbett has lived in London since 2007. She grew up in a low-income area of Liverpool in the 1980s and experienced first-hand a community battling against injustice: at age three, she was squatting with her parents to save local housing from the bulldozer. Sarah is passionate about encouraging people to use their hobbies and talents to be the change they wish to see in the world. She started doing craftivism in 2008 as a hobby and set up the Craftivist Collective in 2009, which now has thousands of supporters across the world. She works with charities such as UNICEF and Save the Children; art institutions such as the Tate and Hayward galleries; and other organizations. She sells products, delivers workshops and talks, and exhibits her craftivism work around the world. She's a columnist for *Crafty Magazine* and the author of *A Little Book of Craftivism*. "A spoonful of craft helps the activism go down" is one of Sarah's favorite sayings. **craftivist-collective.com**, @ **craftivists** (for Instagram & Twitter), and at **etsy.com/shop/craftivistcollective**.

THE CRAFTIVISM MOVEMENT

A phrase coined in 2003 by crafter and author Betsy Greer, craftivism is defined as "a way of looking at life where voicing opinions through creativity makes your voice stronger, your compassion deeper, and your quest for justice more infinite." Craftivism is activism achieved through the act of crafting. *craftivism.com* (To read more, see: Betsy Greer, Craftivism: *The Art and Craft of Activism* (Arsenal Pulp Press, 2014).

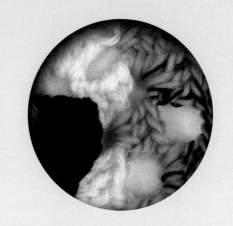

Chapter Five

THE FABRIC OF REMEMBRANCE

We think of our lives—and of stories—as spun threads, extended and knitted or interwoven with others into the fabric of communities, or history, or texts.

—A. S. Byatt in *The Guardian*, **2008**

Memory

Family history isn't hard. We do it every day without thinking about it. Our minds naturally travel in that direction. Our minds are always going home.

—**D. G. Fulford**, *One Memory at a Time: Inspiration & Advice for Writing Your Family Story*

Why commit words onto cloth rather than into the pages of a journal? What makes textiles different than paper? Artists may have many reasons to work with textiles, but often, their love for the medium of fabric has to do with the sense of touch. Through the nap of velvet, the slight roughness of linen, or the silkiness of angora, fabric can evoke memories. Our childhood memories are filled with fabric, from the blankets we were wrapped in to the scratchy sweaters we were forced to wear to school. Quilts, embroideries, and weavings can hold remembrances both personal and collective, and artists can use them to create biographies, autobiographies, genealogies, and memorials.

Traditionally, family genealogies arose from our need to know about our ancestors across vast oceans and through generations of migration and displacement. Few records—but for certificates of birth, border crossings, marriages, and deaths—existed, and these were kept by churches, governments, and schools. Family histories were kept alive through oral storytelling, samplers, and written diaries.

Now that we live in a world of cloud-servers and Instagram, how can we select the important stories that we need to tell? We each have our own ideas of what is important. For some people, traditional life narratives detailing weddings, educational backgrounds, and job titles matter. For others, history is found in unusual souvenirs. Fiber crafts provide a place for experimentation and play, and the stories they tell are often overlooked and unconventional, leaving you with plenty of room to capture your own vision and version of history.

Sherri Lynn Wood, *David Hill (1956–2010) for Quinn and for Sailor,* 2012, machine-pieced, hand-quilted, clothing, 42 x 57 in (106.68 x 144.78 cm). Photo: Sherri Lynn Wood. David was a ship's captain who died at sea saving the lives of his crew members. Sherri Lynn Wood improvised the quilt pattern to create a sense of flowing waves and light on water. David's wife Amy cut apart most of his clothing and sent the pieces to Sherri to make the quilts for his children.

Passage Quilting

Artist Sherri Lynn Wood developed a way to help people who have lost their loved ones process their grief through improvisational quilt-making.

Her method, which she calls Passage Quilting, helps the bereaved repurpose and transform the clothing of lost loved ones into memory quilts to cherish. Sherri facilitates the process of making the quilts, guiding her clients in choosing, piecing, and hand-quilting the clothing, and in sharing their stories. These upcycled materials preserve a sense of the person who has passed and provide consolation.

"Often, people express a fear that they may be overwhelmed by grief, and I remind them that they are simply making a quilt," she says. "This process provides a safe yet active container for sorrow which will enable you to literally touch your grief and stay present to the task at hand."

Sherri Lynn Wood, *Phyllis Jackson (1943–2003)*, 2005, machine-pieced, hand-quilted, clothing, 76 x 78 in (193.04 x 198.12 cm). Photo: Sherri Lynn Wood. Quilt made for Ted Dillingham from his wife Phyllis's evening gowns, everyday dresses, kimono sweaters, coats, lingerie, and wedding clothes, and Ted's wedding scarf and bowtie.

A Memorial in Cloth

"When my father-in-law passed away, I made a textile memorial for our garden. It included words spoken at his memorial service, pictures taken throughout his life, and clothing that he wore. Everything was transferred to fabric to allow me to create prayer flags that would be hung in our garden. I like the Buddhist tradition of the prayer flags—as they disintegrate, the good thoughts and kind messages gently flow into the winds of the world. This was my intent with the flags I made for Ernie Cooper." —Jennifer Cooper

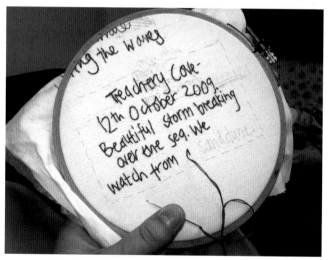

Stitched Travel Diaries

In 2009, UK-based artist Sarah Terry spent a year in Australia as an artist-in-residence at Kinross Wolaroi School in Orange, New South Wales. During her stay she decided to record on cloth her travels around Australia's east coast. She wrote: "I started the diary as a way to explore and record my experiences. I've always been fascinated by creating work that can be directly linked to a certain time or place." Using recycled cotton, thread, and some acetone transfers, Sarah recorded her experiences by hand-stitching her handwriting. "Hand-stitch allowed me the time to meditate on what I was writing and confirm it in my memory, like seeing a thunderstorm breaking over the sea or a whale breaking the waves."

Top: Jennifer Cooper, *A Life Well Lived, A Cloth Memorial for Ernie Cooper*, 2011, cotton, linen, silk, clothing, copper, dimensions unknown. Photo: Jennifer Cooper

Bottom: Sarah Terry works on her stitched diary in Australia, 2009. Photo: Courtesy of Sarah Terry

Exploring Family Genealogy through Stitching

Anne Montgomery's textile project *The Women Before Me* contains photo transfers of her mother as a babe-in-arms with her grandmother, her mother and herself, and her aunt, who passed away when she was just fourteen. The piece includes a silk fusion casting of her grandmother's baby shoe and patches of clothing and linens from previous generations of her family.

"This quilt was a way of imagining a connection between me and my female ancestors. My family was very private, so [when I was growing up] I didn't learn much about their lives, only snippets. Through my work, I am connecting with my personal history."

Anne Montgomery, *The Women Before Me*, 2012, cotton lace and doilies, buttons, children's garments, photo transfers, photo frames, 40 x 28 in (101.6 x 71.12 cm). Photo: Anne Montgomery

CROCHETING JOY:

An Interview with Sayraphim Lothian

As a public artist, Sayraphim Lothian works "in the medium of joy by facilitating playful but meaningful moments between strangers." Through her Moment in Yarn project, she has collected stories on "granny squares" that each contain unique and precious memories. Based in Eaglemont, Australia, her artwork can be found on streets and in pockets around the world. *sayraphimlothian.com*; Twitter: *@sayraphim*; *facebook.com/sayraphimlothian*.

Sayraphim Lothian, *Boudoir*, 2013, acrylic yarn, crochet, 4.72 x 4.72 in (12 x 12 cm). Photo: Sayraphim Lothian

Ever since she had been a young girl
she had always wanted
a boudoir of her own.
A room of serenity
scattered with cushions
and a Turkish rug on the floor

Q: Tell me about *A Moment in Yarn*.

A: It's a project that transforms a participant's happy memory into a granny square in order to generate something tangible from a memory, something a person can take home. I told my partner once that I was worried and upset that I was starting to lose my memories of my late grandmother. My partner suggested that I crochet them into a rug, so I started making granny squares based on what I remembered of my grandmother. It was comforting to have my recollections of her made solid, so they couldn't slip away.

Afterward, I wanted to see if I was able to translate other people's memories into granny squares, so I asked a couple of friends to share memories of their own with me. It was important that my friends could recognize themselves in the final piece. It was heartwarming to see them hold their crocheted square for the first time.

Q: What were some of the stories that were told to you?

A: All kinds of stories! One of the beautiful things about this project is that all people have a need to share. Story-sharing makes people feel like they matter and that the things they have experienced are important to someone else. When I was a primary school teacher, I watched children share stories and beam with pride when they realized that people were listening. Adults need this experience as much as kids.

One of the stories I heard was about how a friend's boyfriend had proposed to her. They were walking along the beach—their favorite spot—when he suddenly dropped to one knee. It was a spontaneous thing, and he didn't have a ring ready. Instead, he offered her a pebble from the beach. That pebble is still one of her most treasured possessions.

Sayraphim Lothian, *Proposal*, 2011, acrylic yarn, crochet, 4.72 x 4.72 in (12 x 12 cm). Photo: Sayraphim Lothian

While walking along the beach
he dropped to one knee
and asked her to marry him.
He didn't have a ring ready
so he offered her a pebble from the sand

Sayraphim Lothian, *The Wedding*, 2011, acrylic yarn, crochet, 4.72 x 4.72 in (12 x 12 cm). Photo: Sayraphim Lothian

The day they were married
they stood on the blanket
(with a tiny red heart in the corner)
the bride's best friend had knitted them
for their housewarming

Sayraphim Lothian, *The New House*, 2011, acrylic yarn, crochet, 4.72 x 4.72 in (12 x 12 cm). Photo: Sayraphim Lothian

They sat on their porch
Eating hot chips
and drinking champagne
as the sun slowly set
on their brand new house

A man told me of the first evening he and his wife spent in their new home, sitting on the porch, eating hot chips, drinking champagne, and watching the sunset over their new front yard. Another friend told me how, as a child, the lady next door looked after her every day while my friend's mum was at work. The lady had a red-and-white checkered table cloth and would cook french fries for her.

Q: Why did you focus on capturing happy memories? Why not all kinds of memories?

A: I think there is a tendency to focus on the bad things in life—everything that's wrong and the things we should be outraged about. I try to balance that out in my work by reminding people of nice experiences. I wanted to give people something they could treasure, and to achieve that goal, the memory needed to be something lovely.

Q: How were the stories told to you?

A: Most were fairly short, a paragraph or two, from which I'd pick specific details to highlight in the crochet. A story of a woman's adventure in a desert oasis in the northern terri-tory [of Australia] was quite long, but it was pretty amusing, and I crocheted while she talked. Sometimes I asked for more detail to help me with the crocheting, and sometimes I liked to just listen to the story.

Q: What strategies did you use to visually convey the story that was told to you?

A: The main strategy was color. I have quite a large stash of yarn, collected over many years, so there are loads of color variations to choose from. I also like to use three-dimensional shapes in the crochet to make more visual connections to the story. One woman asked me to crochet a square as a late wedding gift for a friend who got married standing barefoot on a blanket with a little red heart in the corner. I crocheted the image of the blanket and the heart, and then two gold rings. Granny squares can portray an amazing amount of information, even if they're not a perfect medium!

Getting detail from people is easy; they are always happy to tell you as much as you need about this special story they hold dear. It's a humbling aspect of this project. You don't want to mess with that memory by giving them something crappy based on it. The aim is to make something lovely to accompany the story. ✳

Sayraphim Lothian, *The Fishpond*, 2011, acrylic yarn, crochet, 4.72 x 4.72 in (12 x 12 cm). Photo: Sayraphim Lothian

Two tiny girls
crouched on the small wooden bridge
peering into the murky depths of the fishpond
and are rewarded by
the flash of orange

Prompt

Try Your Hand at Memoir

One of the hardest aspects of writing, particularly memoir writing, can be getting started. If you're having trouble knowing where to begin, try one of these unconventional prompts.

1. Use a tape recorder or a smartphone to record a conversation with a family member. Listen to the conversation when you are alone. What is the subtext of your conversation? This can serve as the beginning of a mini-memoir about your relationship.

2. Do you have a box of keepsakes either from your own past or filled with items handed down to you from a family member? Empty all of the contents onto a large surface and take a look at them. What is the collection comprised of, and what does it tell you about the family?

3. Write about memorable clothes that you've had throughout your life—a pair of patterned socks that you wore to your first day of school, the pants whose broken zipper led to an embarrassing moment, the first booties that you put on your baby. Construct a list of the clothing items you remember owning throughout your life. Don't forget to describe the feel of the fabric, the size of the garment (restrictive or loose and cloud-like?), how it made you feel (elegant or downtrodden, sporty or miserable?) and what you did when you wore each piece.

Here are some techniques to try when creating textiles related to memory:

1. Try to re-create handwriting in stitchwork. From the rough block letters of a child to the elegant script of an older person who had proper penmanship training, handwriting can tell us a lot about a person's character.

2. Collecting photographs and letters (or even emails) and transposing them onto fabric is an effective way of working with items that are photo-realistic without destroying the originals. Digital scans of artwork can be printed using home inkjet printers onto hot-iron fabric transfers.

3. Include fabrics, embellishments, or buttons that have sentimental meaning on your textile art.

4. Collaborate—get others to provide you with quotes, drawings, and facts that you can incorporate into your work.

You want your work to last long into the future—use archival inks and clean textiles, and store your finished work in a moisture- and bug-free place. Who knows? Your creation might last as long as the Bayeux Tapestry.

Paddy Hartley, *Spreckley I & II* (officer uniforms), 2007, digital embroidery, digital fabric print, vintage embroidery, dimensions unknown. Wellcome Collection. Photo: Paddy Hartley.

Paddy Hartley's Project Façade

This unusual project combines art with elements of surgical, social, and military history. Based on materials found in the Gillies Archives, a collection of 2,500 medical records made by pioneering facial surgeon Sir Harold Gillies, *Project Façade* tells the stories of wounded World War I soldiers who were treated for facial reconstruction. Paddy Hartley translates medical records and unearths the pre- and post-operative history of the patients. The stories, relating to the operative techniques of stitching and skin, are then told using embroidery on vintage military uniforms. Since 2004, Hartley has worked on the project in several stages, and new works will appear in 2014–18 to coincide with the centennial of the Great War.

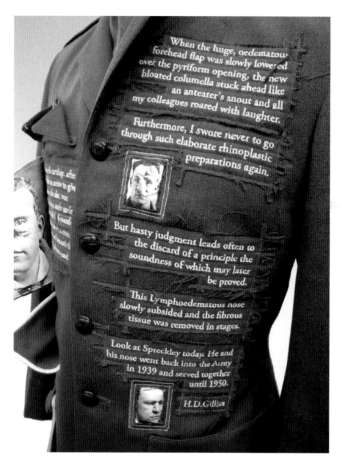

Left & right: Paddy Hartley, detail of *Spreckley I*. The eldest son of a commercial lace-maker, William Michael Spreckley left England for Germany to learn the lace trade in Plauen, near Dresden. While defending Ealing Trench, near Poperinghe [in Belgium], William lost his entire nose to a grenade blast and was subsequently admitted to the Gillies plastic surgery unit back in England. Although the rhinoplastic surgery William underwent had been attempted previously, his was so successful that Gillies noted its significance in the development of nasal reconstruction. Photos: Paddy Hartley

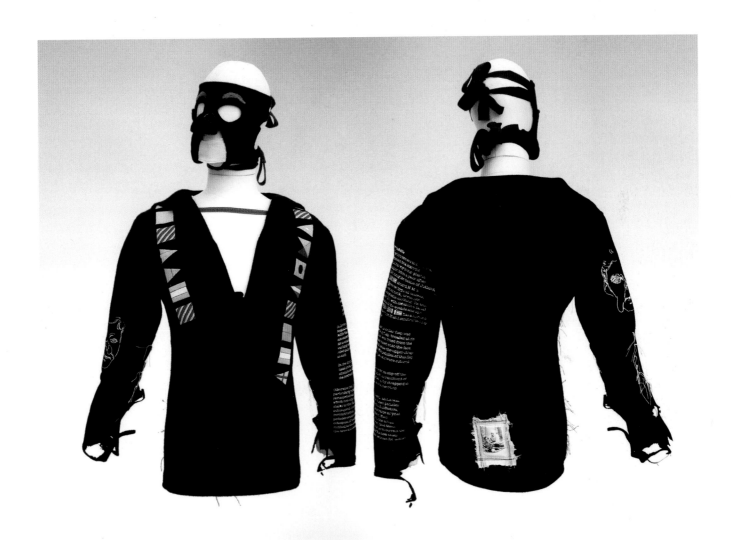

Paddy Hartley, *Vicarage* (sailor uniforms), 2007, digital embroidery, digital fabric print, dimensions unknown. Photo: Paddy Hartley. William Vicarage, a twenty-year-old watchmaker from Swansea, South Wales, suffered serious cordite burns while serving aboard the H.M.S. *Malaya* in the Battle of Jutland. His facial injuries included the loss of most of his nose and part of his ears. Gillies proposed lifting a large "Masonic collar skin flap" from his chest to the lower part of his face. This surgery marked a turning point in skin grafting.

STORY QUILTS:

An Interview with Marion Coleman

Marion Coleman lives in the Castro Valley, California. An internationally exhibiting artist, Marion has been creating her elaborate story quilts for more than twenty-five years. Her quilts are layered pieces of art that include readymade items, photo transfers, and embroidered text. Showing scenes of her community, history, the jazz clubs her relatives visited, or the health care field, Marion's whimsical quilts are engaging and tell the stories of what she sees around her. *marioncoleman.com*

Marion Coleman, *Healing Hands/Caring Hearts*, 2011, cotton, silk upholstery remnants, silk organza, cotton gauze bandages, photo transfers, nursing pledges, fusing, raw edge appliqué, thread writing, machine quilting, 48.5 x 51 in (123.19 x 129.54 cm). Photo: Marion Coleman

Q: How did you get into quilting?

A: I'm from a family of quilters. I have a 103-year-old aunt, who's still living, and she quilted until she was 100. I learned to sew at age five, but it wasn't until I saw African fabric and the opportunity to start putting pictures into quilts that it became exciting to me.

I made my first photo-memory quilt for my mother using African fabrics. From there, I looked to other African-American quilters such as Nora Ezell or Michael Cummings. I really like story quilts. Then, about ten years ago, I had an opportunity to make quilts about the Lewis and Clark Expedition. I knew that there was one African-American on the expedition, and I wanted to tell that story. I've always been fascinated by the work of [documentary filmmaker] Ken Burns. I can't make videos, but I can certainly sew, so I thought I might be able to do it that way. It's been a steady journey. I just keep looking at stories and people and things to make quilts about.

Q: Can you tell me a little bit about the techniques that you use?

A: My 103-year-old aunt had a wonderful stash of old photos. I started to make quilts for family using scans of the photos. I use a photo-transfer with my thirteen by nineteen-inch [33.02 x 48.26-cm] inkjet printer. I free-motion-embroidery words, and sometimes I collage words and statements into quilts. I use silk and cotton and sometimes also add old clothes, and just about anything I can think of.

Q: *Healing Hands/Caring Hearts* is about nursing history. How did that piece come about?

A: If I find a photo that reminds me of something, then I start looking for whatever I can find to help me visualize the story I want to tell about it. I have a collection of old photos of nurses, so I started to research them. I'm from the segregated south. I'm old enough to have gone to an all-black high school in Texas, and I remember having black-only health practitioners back then. Using the images, I researched the professional organizations that the nurses belonged to. From being in the social services myself, I knew that the nurses played an important role in prenatal care. The nurses probably would have gone to people's houses as midwives to deliver babies because blacks were not allowed to go to white hospitals.

I'm not telling any particular story—it's every story; it's about every nurse. I want the viewer to have a sense of what they might have been like. It's important to me that all those women before me, who didn't have the opportunities that I had, have some recognition of their place in history and what they've done and experienced. Sometimes it's joyful, sometimes not. What's important to me as a woman who's over sixty-five is acquainting a new generation with what life was like.

Q: What is the story of the work called *Angry Young Men*?

A: I did *Angry Young Men* in collaboration with my son, who'll be thirty-four soon. I love to talk with him about his experiences of being black and American and a certain age. He's very honest, and he polls his friends for me and tells me how they're feeling about things.

[This quilt] tells a story about how [these young men are] very angry and what can create that anger. Sometimes they

Marion Coleman, detail *Healing Hands/Caring Hearts*, 2011, cotton, silk upholstery remnants, silk organza, cotton gauze bandages, photo transfers, nursing pledges, fusing, raw edge appliqué, thread writing, machine quilting, 48.5 x 51 in (123.19 x 129.54 cm). Photo: Marion Coleman

NORA EZELL (1917–2007)

was a quilter renowned for her narrative quilts. Her colorful and abstract pieces commemorated key historical events and figures, including Dr Martin Luther King, the civil-rights era in Alabama, and Native American history.

Marion Coleman, *Angry Young Men*, 2006, cotton, photo transfers, fusing, raw edge appliqué, thread writing, machine quilting, 49.5 x 47 in (125.73 x 119.38 cm). Photo: Marion Coleman. A social commentary on violence, the criminal-justice system, and community ambivalence on the loss of a generation of young adults.

have young mothers, they may have absent fathers, they've missed a lot of school—they're never really going to be able to catch up. Maybe they're frustrated because they don't have any skills or because they're always suspect. They can just be walking down the street and be in the wrong place. I was reminded of when I had just moved to Oakland [in the 1970s], a couple of blocks from an upscale neighborhood called Piedmont. I went walking in my own neighborhood, just getting acquainted with it, and a police officer stopped and asked me if I was lost. I thought, See, here it is. I was reminded that we still have a long way to go, and that's what *Angry Young Men* is about.

Q: Can you tell me about *Saturday Night Rhythms*?

A: That was made for a Carolyn Mazloomi show about jazz quilts, called *Textural Rhythms*. It shows my family going to a jazz club. The guy with the hat is my cool uncle Matt. The woman wearing the white dress is my mom, who likes to sing. I had some old shots of families in juke joints. I called it *Saturday Night Rhythms* because it's Saturday night, but then, of course, the next morning they dress up and go to church.

It's a jazz theme, but I'm not showing Louis Armstrong or Nina Simone or other well-known people; I'm showing the audience. I did another piece called *A Sound of Their Own* that focused on the background singers, who are always keeping the rhythm going, but we don't necessarily know their names. We know it might be Ella Fitzgerald in the front and just that somebody in the back is doo-wopping right along. ✳

Top: Marion Coleman, *Textual Rhythms Series: Saturday Night Rhythm*, 2005, pieced, layered, stitched textiles with manipulated photo transfers, 36 x 38.5 in (92 x 97.79 cm). Photos: Marion Coleman

Bottom: detail, Marion Coleman, *Textual Rhythms Series: Saturday Night Rhythm*, 2005, pieced, layered, stitched textiles with manipulated photo transfers, 36 x 38.5 in (92 x 97.79 cm). Photos: Marion Coleman

Project

I Love My City Tote Bag

LINDSAY ZIER-VOGEL

In 2004, Lindsay Zier-Vogel started *The Love Lettering Project,* an example of community arts engagement. The I Love My City tote is a way to tell everyone on the street or in the coffee shop what you love about your city and inspire them to do the same.

Note: This project can be adapted by embroidering an existing tote bag.

Create Your Story
Think of something that you love about the city where you live. Maybe it's the flower vendor on a favorite street corner or the feeling you have when you're in a certain neighborhood. Maybe it's the view from the waterfront, or the skyline, or a certain stretch of road. Whatever it is, write it a letter!

Here are a few examples:

Dear City,
I love that you are covered in the coziest blanket every winter.
xoxo

Dear City,
I love how you shine at night.
xoxo

Dear City,
I love your unending parks.
xoxo

TOOLS & MATERIALS

- 14.96 x 18.11 in (38 x 46 cm) cotton twill (outer fabric)

- 14.96 x 18.11 in (38 x 46 cm) cotton fabric (liner fabric)

- 1 spool thread, to match twill

- 2 19.7 x 1.5 in (50 x 3.81 cm) pieces of cotton webbing, for tote handles*

- OR, a ready-made blank tote bag

- 2 skeins embroidery floss

- size 4 embroidery needle

- 7 in (17.78 cm) wooden embroidery hoop (or smaller)

- scissors

- pencil

- white eraser

- straight pins

- iron

- ruler

*For these, Lindsay used pre-made thick cotton webbing (like this: *https://www.etsy.com/listing/90279102/ cotton-bag-handle-black-cotton-webbing?ref=market*)

SKILLS

basic embroidery
basic machine sewing (unless using a readymade tote bag)

PATTERN NOTES

Finished dimensions are 13.19 x 13.78 in (33.5 x 35 cm) and 3.54 in (9 cm) deep

- Pre-wash and dry fabric.

- With a pencil, write the love letter in the center of twill fabric, leaving at least 2.36 in (6 cm) at top and at least 3.94 in (10 cm) at the bottom. If using an existing tote bag, center text in the middle of the bag.

- Using all six strands of embroidery floss, chain stitch around penciled text. Trim loose threads and iron out embroidery-hoop crease marks. If using an existing tote, you're done! If sewing your own tote bag, proceed to the next step.

☞ Optional

Sew the tote bag

Make the lining:

    Pin together 2 pieces of liner material with right sides facing. Using a sewing machine with a 0.5-in (1.27-cm) seam allowance, stitch along one side, turn onto bag bottom, and turn again, sewing up the other side.

    Pinch corner and line up the side seams so that corner fabric makes a triangle. Measure 2.95 in (7.5 cm) from corner and draw a perpendicular line with pencil. Sew along that line, keeping side seams open. Complete both liner corners and cut off extra fabric.

    Keep tote inside out and pin 1.57-in (4-cm) seam from open edge of bag.

Sew the outer bag

Pin together 2 pieces of twill with right sides facing. Using a sewing machine with a 0.5-in (1.27-cm) seam allowance, stitch both sides of the bag and the bottom.

Pinch corner and line up side seams so that corner fabric makes a triangle. Measure 3.15 in (8 cm) from corner and draw a perpendicular line with pencil. Sew along that line, keeping side seams open. Complete both corners and cut off extra fabric.

Flip fabric right-side out and pin a 1.57-in (4-cm) seam from open edge of bag.

☞ Finishing

Slide lining inside outer shell and pin corners together. Pin handle fabric to twill 3.93 in (10 cm) from edge of bag, with 3.93 in (10 cm) between each end of handle. Pin outer fabric to inner fabric. Be careful to tuck handle tops down into bag. Sew through all layers at the top of the bag, keeping handles sandwiched between the lining and the outside twill. Trim loose threads.

Your city love letter bag is complete!

Lindsay Zier-Vogel is a writer, arts educator, book maker, and creator of *The Love Lettering Project* (LLP). Since 2004, she has been asking people to write love letters to their cities, slip them into airmail envelopes addressed to "love," and distribute them anonymously throughout their communities to be discovered by strangers. After a fourteen-event tour of Toronto in the summer of 2013, she took the project on a five-city tour of the UK, funded in part by the Canada Council for the Arts. To celebrate the tenth anniversary of the project, she went on a three-city tour of Canada's Far North in 2014. *lindsayziervogel.com; loveletteringproject.com*

Chapter Six

ILLUSTRATIVE STORYTELLING

The history of storytelling through creations on cloth works around the need for words. There are all kinds of pictorial storytelling traditions.

—textile artist, poet, and professor Maria Damon

A visual conversation

My work is not about beauty. It is about life. Blood. Angst.
Energy to the maximum.

—*Consuelo Jimenez Underwood,*
an artist who constructs histories of Indigenous peoples' conflicts through weaving

Not all stories are told in the form of words. Symbols, illustrations, signs, gestures, icons, images, and maps can relate visual meaning to a reader. From a single picture that causes a viewer to ask questions to a series of pictograms that communicate the psychology of a society, images, just like written stories, are created with the intention of reaching another person. The presence of an image encourages you to decode it in order to respond with your own story. You may wonder what led to the making of an image and what resulted from its creation. Pictures can also convey emotion—you don't need to read the words "sad," "angry," or "happy"; you experience these feelings just by looking at the piece. Textile artists, such as the ones featured in this chapter, use representative imagery to explore all kinds of stories.

Button Blankets

On Canada's west coast, the traditional ceremonial button blankets and thick knitted Cowichan sweaters of the Coast Salish peoples include story designs. The Coast Salish heritage is rooted deeply in oral storytelling traditions, and the blankets and sweaters of these peoples often contain imagery of animals—ravens, beavers, hummingbirds, eagles, or whales—to signify family and clan stories. Button blankets are often made of wool and traditionally were adorned with mother-of-pearl buttons in a design that denoted the wearer's family or clan.

In contemporary times, the button blanket is still worn to feasts or potlatches among the peoples of the north Pacific coast. The Haida, Tsimshian, Tlingit, and Nisga'a peoples all wear button blankets. Contemporary artists Delores Churchill, Evelyn Vanderhoops, Jennifer Annaïs Pighin, and Dorothy Grant are reinventing traditional blanket designs with modern re-interpretations.

In Northwest tradition and etiquette, each symbol and its design belongs to one family, and only they have the right to tell their stories verbally and through their art. To be given a blanket or a sweater adorned with these designs and told their stories is an honor, and one that can only be bestowed by someone of Coast Salish heritage.

Jennifer Annaïs Pighin, *Beaver Button Blanket/Tsa Nanezmaz Nalhti*, 2005, melton cloth, yarn, and nickels, 5 x 4.5 ft (1.52 x 1.37 m). Photo: Jennifer Annaïs Pighin

Jennifer Annaïs Pighin's *Beaver Button Blanket*

"This handmade button blanket, made in the fashion of the traditional ceremonial Northwest Coast First Nations robes, is for a member of the beaver clan who understands the insignificance of money and true history of the nation. The image of the beaver also represents the strong, diligent nature of this magnificent creature. One must remember the value of all creatures on our planet as they each play a crucial role in maintaining balance in our ecology. We also must remember that we have much to learn from their instincts and actions. When we look to the beaver for guidance, we find a strong-willed, studious being with great architectural skills whose work benefits and nurtures all living creatures and the surrounding environment for miles around. The beaver's building materials consist of wood and earth. It uses them wisely, not wasting a twig. Our society could learn from such resourcefulness, especially since our economy and livelihood greatly rely on trees and earth.

The significance of using nickels [on the blanket] reflects our current value system in a few ways, one of which is the fact that, in Canada, trade values were originally measured in beaver pelts, and the beaver's image is used on the nickel.

The nickel coin is a form of money made from the refined mineral nickel, mined from the earth. Resource extraction has generated much debate between the First Nations of this land and the Europeans who have taken control of it regarding land usage and environmental impacts of mining. The management of the environment, resources, and all earths' inhabitants warrants serious consideration...By drilling holes through these nickels, I render them 'worthless' for consumer purposes. This blanket serves as a bold statement toward redefining value."

....

Jennifer Annaïs Pighin is an accomplished visual artist and educator living in Prince George, British Columbia. She is a proud member of the Lheidli T'enneh First Nation, with Wet'suwet'en, French Canadian, and Italian ancestry. A graduate student at the University of Northern British Columbia, Jennifer holds a BA in Visual Arts from Emily Carr University and a Bachelor of Education with a specialization in art from the University of British Columbia. As a secondary school teacher, she received the Prince George Regional Arts & Culture Award for Education in 2012 and was nominated for the Aboriginal Woman of Distinction Award in 2009. These accomplishments are testament to her commitment, volunteerism, and various contributions to the community. Rooted within the community, Jennifer's artwork is often collaborative in nature. It uses a wide range of media, including painting, drawing, digital design, mosaic, traditional arts, and public installations. Her work was showcased in the Canada Pavilion at the 2008 Summer Olympics in Beijing and is currently featured within the branding of the 2015 Canada Winter Games. *jenniferannaispighin.com*

APPROACH A STORY THROUGH IMAGERY

- If you're working with a series of images, remember that all stories have a beginning, middle, and end. What is the beginning, middle, and end of your story, and which single picture would you choose to represent each stage?

- What is the climax of the story? Challenge yourself to look beyond it. What is a quiet moment in the story that tells just as much about the characters, feeling, and setting? Try showing this quiet moment in a single image.

- How can you tell a well-known story from a different perspective? How would a child or an animal approach the situation? What if the antagonist appeared likable? What if the story was told from the perspective of the opposite gender? How would it look from a bird's-eye view?

STRANGER THAN FICTION:
An Interview with Freddie Robins

Internationally renowned UK-based artist Freddie Robins creates work that challenges the perception of knitting and craft in the context of the visual art world. She studied textiles at Middlesex University (previously Polytechnic) and the Royal College of Art before establishing her own design company Tait & Style. In 1997, she turned to creating conceptually focused textile pieces. From her infamous work *Craft Kills* (see p. 18) to recreated three-dimensional knitted models of the homes where Victorian female serial killers did their work, Robin's work is wryly observant of society's fascination with sensationalism and our attitudes towards fear, gender, and even language.

Freddie Robins, Catherine Long wears *AT ONE*, 2001, machine-knitted wool, hand-embroidered cotton yarn, 18.11 x 15.75 in (46 x 40 cm).
Photo: Freddie Robins

Q: There is a lot of wordplay in your work. How does language fit into your artistic practice?

A: Normally I use it as a way to generate ideas—I turn it into a game, rhyming and changing letters within words. I also enjoy the use of words in textiles that I make, and I incorporate words into my knitting. I like the interchange of images and words.

Wordplay formed the basis of two commissions I made for, and in conjunction with, Mat Fraser and Catherine Long. Strong, confrontational wording with an element of humor and the unexpected. Disabilities have long been the butt of jokes. I wanted to turn these jokes and sayings upside down. With Mat, who has short arms, we also wanted to challenge the commonly held assumption that disabled people are passive and somehow harmless. I originally had the wording "armless and dangerous" in mind, a play on the phrase "armed and dangerous." Mat is far from harmless but, as he corrected me, he is not armless either. He is, in fact, short-armed and dangerous. This exactness of language is very important. It is not about political correctness, it is about thinking, caring, and acceptance.

Catherine has one arm—she does not have only one arm. The word "only" implies some kind of loss or deficiency, which is far from the truth. We used the word ONE on both her sweater and glove. Her glove has the word ONE embroidered across the knuckles, where you might see the words "love" or "hate" tattooed. When she holds her clenched fist up and flicks out her thumb, it shows the word UP embroidered on it. She is ONE-UP. The tattoo theme was taken into her sweater, which has a butterfly and a bunch of daisies embroidered onto her shoulder; these are symbols that have significant personal meaning for Catherine. There is a banner running through the daisies that reads AT ONE. She is one with her arm; why aren't you?

Q: In 1999, you took a public commission from the London Borough of Hackney for Shoreditch Library in which you created a series of knitted gloves to represent local history and parts of the institution. Can you tell me about your Hands of Hoxton project?

A: They requested an installation that highlighted different aspects of the library and the things that a community might like to do there. I researched stories of the local area and discovered a whole range of different characters, whom I decided to link to the different functions of the library. The project is very multi-layered, and I conveyed the information through installation cases with the gloves and interpretative panels with line drawings, so the viewer can see the glove and read the corresponding story. Each glove is named after an individual and each story relates to a particular function of the library. For example, the piece called *Kate Greenaway* has fingers that are joined, so it looks like your hands are a book, to tell you that the library has story-time sessions for children.

Q: You've frequently used gloves as a tool for communication. Can you tell me about Conrad in your Odd Gloves series?

A: Conrad is a character who has his thumb cut off. He's from the Der Struwwelpeter [Shockheaded Peter] stories, German cautionary tales for children. Conrad was told not to suck his thumbs or a tailor would cut them off. Of course,

Freddie Robins, Mat Fraser wears *SHORT ARMED AND DANGEROUS*, 2000, machine-knitted wool, 28.74 x 18.90 in (73 x 48 cm).
Photo: Freddie Robins

Freddie Robins, *Hands of Hoxton* Installation, 1999, machine and
hand-knitted yarn in acrylic cases. Photo: Jamie Thompson

THE STORIES BEHIND THE GLOVES

(Top row, left to right)

Thomas

All library members have access to the business library. During the seventeenth century, Hoxton was renowned for its "green fingers" [i.e., green thumbs]. Thomas Fairchild was the greatest of the Hoxton market and nursery gardeners. He was a prosperous businessman and, had he been alive today, he could further his success through use of the business library.

James

This library holds local and national information on health. By the nineteenth century, Hoxton had become home to a number of private lunatic asylums. James Parkinson was a local doctor who lived at 1 Hoxton Square. He initiated many improvements and pressed for the humane treatment of the patients treated within these asylums. The illness known as Parkinson's disease is named in honor of him, as he identified it in 1817.

Kate

There is a children's library, which includes books for the under-fives. This library also has a textbook and homework collection to help children with their schoolwork. Kate Greenaway (1846–1901), the famous writer and illustrator of children's books, was born at 1 Cavendish Street in Hoxton.

(Middle row, left to right)

Henry

This library has local and national newspapers and holds information about what's on. In the nineteenth century, Shoreditch had its own special Sunday-morning bird market in Sclater Street. Henry Busby Bird was a notable local politician in the early twentieth century. "A bird in the hand is worth two in the bush."

Lakshmi

This library stocks information on world faiths and can supply information about local places of worship. Lakshmi is the Hindu goddess of wealth and good fortune.

Peter

This library holds storytelling sessions for children. Captain James Hook is Peter Pan's adversary in J.M. Barrie's classic children's story *Peter Pan*.

Caroline

This library is free to join and there is no charge for borrowing books. Thumbs up is the hand signal for "good."

(Bottom row, left to right)

David

This library works "hand in glove" with other libraries to give you access to books and information held there. David was the head librarian at Shoreditch Library (in 1999).

Andrew

This library provides access to the Internet for all its members. These gloves represent the single-hand alphabet sign for "WWW" (World Wide Web).

All gloves were machine-knitted by Freddie Robins except for Thomas, which was hand-knitted by Jean Arkell.

Top: Freddie Robins, *Hands of Hoxton*, 1999, machine- and hand-knitted yarn in acrylic cases, 35.43 x 47.24 x 3.94 in (90 x 120 x 10 cm). Photo: Jamie Thompson. A public commission by the London Borough of Hackney for Shoreditch Library.

Bottom: Freddie Robins, *Knitted Homes of Crime*, 2002, hand-knitted wool, quilted lining fabric. Photo: Douglas Atfield

Conrad did, and he lost his thumbs. Odd Gloves was a very direct interpretation of these cautionary tales, which I've always really loved because they're so hideous and cruel. I've always been interested in the dark side. I think that has something to do with wanting to unpick things that other people aren't prepared to talk to about. I'm interested in dealing with things that are difficult and confronting things that are really terrifying.

Q: Tell me about the *Knitted Homes of Crime* series.

A: I created this series when I was doing a lot of work with feminism and gender inequality. I was fascinated to find that women face prejudice even in crime. They are doubly damned for committing a murder: once for committing the murder, once for daring to go "against" their sex. It fascinated me that there was nothing good recorded about these women, and [what is recorded about them is] often quite derogatory. I'd been collecting these stories for quite a long time. I also had a collection of hideous hand-knitted items— lumpy, ugly things, including a lot of tea cozies. These ideas came together in one of those magical moments: "Oh my god, this is the way to talk about these ideas! This is the format they should take."

I've got quite a few books on murderers, and one of them has the addresses and images of houses [where murders were committed]. I went [to look at the houses], took photographs [of them], and turned them into knitting patterns. The series also brings up issues with women killing in different ways than men do. Women, for example, generally do not kill spontaneously because they lack physical strength. I found a saying, "When poison is found, the murderer is gowned." Poison is the murder weapon of choice for women. When the project was finished, I took an adult education course called "Murder in Our Midst" because I became so intrigued in this whole notion of killing, of socially, emotionally, and humanly unacceptable behavior. I've always fantasized about being a detective, like Miss Marple with her knitting.

Q: The pieces in your *Odd Gloves* series are so visually appealing, but if someone was to pull them off the gallery wall, most of them couldn't be worn.

A: I studied as a designer, so *Odd Gloves* came to me from a remark that I made about not making design-based objects anymore. They were objects to be seen, to be talked about, to be thought about, but not to go on the body. I think the minute you do something functional, it has to have a cost; it has to be affordable. I wanted to avoid that. I also didn't want to get involved in trying to make production lines of things, or things that had to fit people—I wanted to leave those practical considerations out of the equation.

My new work has a lot to do with death and fear and loss. Cheery subjects! I have been looking at how, in other cultures, death is talked about, handled, and celebrated. I am inspired by the decorative skeletons of central Europe, where the corpse and skeleton are adorned. I found this type of embellishment interesting. Making beautiful things is quite unfashionable in the art world. I am interested in how I could use sequins and pretty things with body parts and limbs. Although it's a very dark subject, I'm trying to embrace it and have fun with it, with the conflicting [themes] within the work.

Freddie Robins with *Styllou* from the Knitted Homes of Crime series.
Photo: Peter Sharpe

Freddie Robins, *The Saddest Sight of All*, 2008 antique mirror, mixed media. Installed at PM Gallery & House, London.
Photo: Ben Coode-Adams

Q: What inspired *The Saddest Sight of All*?

A: It's a small installation with woodpeckers that tells the story of girl who died when she fell off the roof of our old house. After she died, a woodpecker came down our chimney and pecked its reflection in the mirror until it died. I didn't witness the girl dying, but I did experience the tragedy because she fell off the roof of the flat above us. I always had this feeling that I would come home one day and find her family in mourning in our front garden. I was always haunted by the fact that they never came, or at least I never saw them. I suppose this piece of work exorcised my thoughts about why the family didn't come to the house. This piece obviously taps into the ongoing theme that I have with death, with staring death in the face. I liked the way I was able to bring these two stories together. ✳

EXPLORING INTERNAL AND EXTERNAL GEOGRAPHIES:

An Interview with Bettina Matzkuhn

As the Canadian child of German immigrants, Bettina Matzkuhn grew up learning how to make things at an early age, and she says that the experience "shaped me in terms of thrift." She created three award-winning films for Canada's National Film Board in the early 1980s using animated textiles. Bettina holds a BFA in Visual Arts and an MFA in Liberal Studies from Simon Fraser University. She has worked with fiber for more than thirty years with an emphasis on embroidery and fabric collage, and narrative continues to inform her work, as evidenced by her love of language and keen interest in human behavior.

Bettina Matzkuhn, *The Magic Quilt*. The quilt was created by Bettina for her short film *The Magic Quilt* (National Film Board of Canada), 1985. Photo: Bettina Matzkuhn

Q: You've made several films involving animated textiles for Canada's National Film Board (NFB). Can you tell me about the experience of animating fiber?

A: In many ways, that was my apprenticeship. I had to figure out how to manipulate textiles to make something happen under the camera. When you make films, you create a narrative. You make a storyboard where you have to plot out what you are going to do. When I was attending college, I started making things out of fabric—it was my language. I could express myself by creating things.

At the end of my degree, I made a hand-drawn film in which I added a part, just to use the last five seconds of film, with a quilt that I had made. After I moved back to Vancouver, I had the tenacity to walk into the NFB and ask if I could work with them! They asked for samples of my work and I showed one of the producers the awful film. When he saw the quilt, he said that they had an experimental budget, and perhaps there was something that we could do with the quilt ... At the same time, I was working as a summer student for Circle Craft, a local artisan gallery, where I was inspired by the glass, ceramics, and weavings there. I started making small embroideries, entering exhibits, and selling at Christmas markets.

Now, I occasionally make the odd smaller piece as a sketch, but I sink my energies into the larger works that interest me. I like to think of it as illustrating my own life.

Q: You work a lot with imagery of sails and boating.

A: My dad was a sailor. When he died a few years ago, I had this idea of making big sails that would be caught in mid-motion. I did a lot of research about the kinds of sails and the type of imagery that appears on sails. I thought

Bettina Matzkuhn, *Tides*, 2011, cotton canvas, hand embroidery, cotton thread, machine-sewn sails, hand-worked corners/grommets, sisal rope, stainless steel tubing, assorted nautical fittings, formed wooden battens, cut plate-steel bases, 12 x 9 x 4 ft (360 x 270 x 120 cm). Photo: Bettina Matzkuhn

about how my dad could read tide charts as easy as you and I can read *Dick and Jane*. He knew the meanings of the symbols on the charts…I made one sail that was comprised of old patches; some of the "windjammers" kept patching their sails when they were away on the water, as they couldn't get new material. Then I started to get into weather symbols. The minute that I saw them, I thought, I'm going to start embroidering these. The periods symbolize rain, the S-like signs are sandstorms, and the six-sided shapes are snowflakes. I thought that these were like writing. I'm reorganizing the stitched symbols to make sentences. I think it will be fun to see how people respond to it. I have an innate curiosity, and I like to learn about new things. Once you start research, you begin to see more and more. I am interested in the semiotics of how things acquire meaning and how they submit meaning.

Q: How did you come up with the idea to make *The Adjectival Coast*?

A: I was looking at historical nautical maps. I like symbolic systems and their history. I'd recently had some life upheaval; these maps are about finding one's way and orienting oneself. I am inspired by a lot of maps from the 1500s and 1600s. The explorers knew and mapped settlements, but when they didn't know what lay inland, they just made it up. When you meet a person, you form impressions using adjectives—that person is aggressive or pompous or whatever. Despite this, you don't really know what is further inland; the aggressive person might be a teddy bear. You won't really know until you get to know them. I started to collect adjectives, and the staff at the library where I work

Bettina Matzkuhn, *The Adjectival Coast*, 2007, fabric paint and hand embroidery,
52 x 44 in (132 x 112 cm). Photo: Bettina Matzkuhn

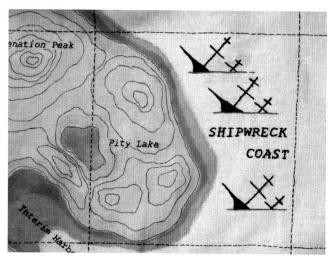

Top & Bottom: Bettina Matzkuhn, details of *The Romantic Archipelago*.
Photos: Bettina Matzkuhn

found words for me. They came up with all sorts of good adjectives like "feckless" and "smarmy." I printed out the words backward and used a blending marker to transfer them onto fabric with acetone, and then I painted it with fabric dye. Then I started embroidering the letters. The words accumulated, just like the mapping process. You bump into a new shore, you meet the natives, and you do or don't make friends.

Some of the old maps have wild cartouches, and they usually have a resident sea monster or two. I've put these kinds of creatures on *The Romantic Archipelago*—there's a unicorn dog and a sabre-tooth bunny. A friend of mine gave me a book about decorative maps that she found in a used bookstore. It inspired me to wonder, What if the cartouche takes over the map? Cartouches carry so much meaning in terms of what people thought were decorative or important.

Q: Tell me about the fabric scroll that you made on your trip to the Yukon.

A: Often, if you don't show someone a photograph [of your travels], it is almost like it didn't happen. I don't have photographs, but I know exactly how I felt at every moment because I was drawing it and recording it on a spool of fabric. Before I left, I prepped the spool by marking it with a line at every centimeter. Each centimeter represents a kilometer [0.62 miles]. I unrolled it as I traveled and drew on it every day with a waterproof pen. When I came home, I started embroidering in my drawings. I display this on stands of plumbing pipe, and I loop it through the gallery to see the whole thing at once. It forms a little landscape of its own; it's like I'm telling you a story as you look at it. But as you look at it, you are making up your own story. I think that is the nature of human experience. ✳

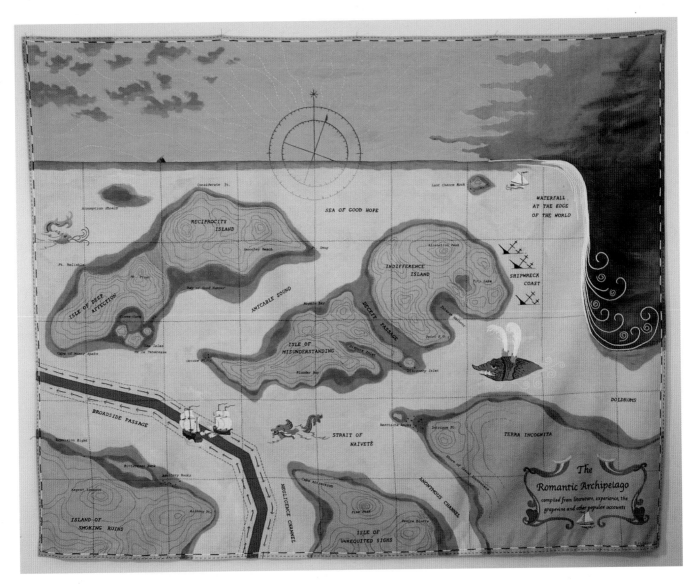

Bettina Matzkuhn, *The Romantic Archipelago*. Photo: Bettina Matzkuhn

Project

Treasure Map

AMANDA WOOD

Amanda Wood's interest in collecting was re-kindled when her five-year-old started collecting things in their neighborhood. Watching his face light up each time he found a dirty, rusted bottle cap in the gutter reminded her of her own childhood collecting habits. Other people's castoffs were her treasure. She wanted to remember this magical time in her son's life, so by mapping his collecting moments and including a little bit of his writing, she created a very personal portrait of his fleeting five-year-old self.

What's Your Story?

Think of meaningful experiences or memories that can be put on a map. For inspiration, take a look at city maps and explore the shapes and lines within them. Consider imagery that could work within the map structure or would contrast well with it. What do you treasure? It could be something as simple as your favorite books placed on a map of good places to read, your daily commute and the snacks you eat on the way, or the houses that you lived in as a child. Have fun playing with the scale of objects and memory. Make it as unique and as eccentric as you are!

TOOLS & MATERIALS

- 4–5 skeins six-strand embroidery floss (assorted colors, see below)

- 32 x 22 in (81.28 x 55.8 cm) neutral light colored linen (1 yd/1 m). **Note**: The first measurement is the size needed to complete the project. The second measurement is a suggestion for what to buy at the fabric store to allow a little extra for testing pigments.

- 32 x 22 (81.28 x 55.8 cm) heavy fabric (lightweight wool, linen, or cotton-linen blend) (1 yd/1 m)

- 31 x 21 in (78.74 x 53.34 cm) buckram (1 yd/1 m)

- Chartpak blender marker

- 3 1.52-oz (45-mL) bottles fabric paint (red, yellow, blue)

- 1 roll 1-in (2.5-cm) masking tape

- HB pencil

- 3–5 sheets letter-sized tracing paper

- embroidery or small sewing scissors

- assorted embroidery needles

- 12-in (30-cm) embroidery hoop

- bone folder or old spoon

- small acrylic paintbrush

- sewing machine

- iron and ironing board

- dry-toner based photocopier

- overhead projector (optional)

SKILLS

- basic machine sewing

- basic embroidery skills (backstitch, French knot, satin stitch)

- drawing skills

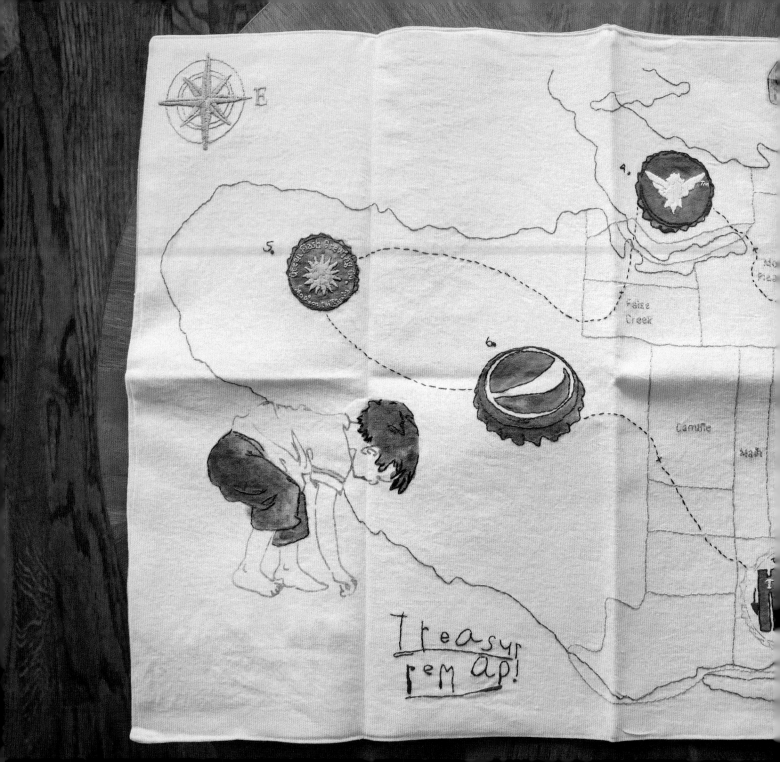

☞ Create images

Choose a city map. Look for an interesting and relevant section to work with. Do some drawing or search for pictures that represent your collection. Trace over them and then add personal details. Create more than you think you need. Think about all five senses and search for images that work well together in terms of shape or color. Don't worry about scale. Visual interest is often achieved by altering the scale of familiar items. If you'd like include a compass rose, you can copy and trace the one (p. 146) onto your own map.

Play with the images to create a balanced visual composition that works within the map. Use a photocopier or scanner to get them to the right size. Use masking tape to mark out a 32 x 22-in (81.28 x 55.88-cm) rectangle on your work surface in which you can lay out the printed images to test how they look together.

The map should be large enough to fill the majority of the space, leaving 2 in (5.08 cm) around the edges for seam allowance (and a little extra). At this point, think about making it larger or smaller to make the images work well. Keep in mind that the images will transfer in reverse. This is especially important if using text. Use a photocopier or computer software such as Adobe Illustrator to create a mirror image.

☞ Transfer images

Pre-wash and dry fabric and cut to size.

If using an overhead projector, create transparencies with a marker or photocopier. Tape linen fabric to a wall. Line up projector so that image is projected onto fabric. Use a pencil to trace the lines. This works well for larger, less detailed images such as the outlines of the map. For more complex images, make photocopies and use the solvent-transfer method described below:

- To transfer with solvent, make copies of all images at correct size. It is very important to use a photocopier that uses dry toner. Ink-based printers and photocopiers will not work. The solvent in the marker dries quickly and the image transfer happens while it is still wet. Gather together the masking tape, bone folder (or old spoon), Chartpak blender pen, pencil, and photocopies so that all the transfer supplies are within reach.

- Tape the 32 x 22-in (81.28 x 55.88-cm) piece of linen to a board or protected surface. If weather permits, do this outside. **CAUTION**: If working inside, do this in a well-ventilated workspace, or open the windows. Wear a mask to avoid inhaling toxic vapors.

- Use masking tape to secure photocopied images face-down onto the linen, placed where you want to transfer them. Make sure tape does not cover any of the transfer area. Draw a rough 1-in (2.5-cm) square (about the size of a postage stamp) on the back of the taped-down photocopy. Fill in the square with the blender pen, and then rub it with the back of the bone folder or old spoon. **CAUTION**: Do not use the spoon with food after using it to transfer images!

- Repeat this process until the entire image has been covered with solvent and rubbed. Remove paper and tape. The toner from the photocopies will have transferred to the fabric. The blender pen will dry out quickly so transfer only small areas at a time and replace marker cap when not using.

Amanda Wood. Compass Rose

☞ Color your story

Spend some time thinking about colors. One approach is to create a restricted palette of about 3–5 colors for a simple, clean look. Try coloring in photocopies to see how the colors will look together. Create the final palette by mixing the three primary-color pigments (or purchase pigments in pre-mixed colors). It is helpful to paint a bit of pigment on a scrap of fabric for color-matching reference. Keep a record of the brand and dye lot number of the floss as well.

☞ Apply pigment and heat-set

Consider painting in the larger areas that would be challenging or very time-consuming to embroider. It's not necessary to add color everywhere.

Dilute mixed pigment with a little water. Test the consistency of pigment on a scrap of fabric before painting on the map. A nice effect is a watercolor-like finish that soaks into the fabric, but at a thicker consistency, it can look more like an acrylic that sits on top. Either way works fine.

Fill in images with pigment. It will bleed a little on the fabric, so paint just inside the lines. In this project, Amanda created a child-like map and wanted to capture the essence of childhood by coloring outside the lines.

Follow the instructions for heat setting that come with pigment. Let pigment air dry for at least 24 hours, and then heat-set it with a household dryer on "hot" for 1 hour. Cover piece with a pressing cloth, then iron design with a very hot, dry iron for about 5–10 minutes to give it a final set.

☞ Embellishment

Using 2–3 threads of floss, add details to the map with embroidery. Backstitch or stem stitch are good for outlining, satin stitch for filling in larger areas, and decorative stitches for borders or text. Amanda's project uses just backstitch and satin stitch with a few French knots.

👉 Put it all together

Gently press map on back. Check size and placement of embroidery. Trim any excess and cut backing fabric to match. Line up backing fabric with right sides together, pinning along all 4 edges. On a sewing machine, sew all 4 sides together with a 0.75-in (2-cm) seam allowance, leaving a 2–3-in (5–7-cm) opening on one side.

Trim corners at an angle to reduce bulk and turn it right-side out. Use a hot iron to create a crisp, even edge. Tuck buckram inside, and iron once more to make sure it fits nicely without bulging at the edges. Trim it slightly if needed.

Topstitch 0.125 in (3 mm) from edge all around to close up opening and secure buckram. To create the folds of the map: Fold the map in quarters like an accordion, horizontally across, ironing each fold separately, then fold in half vertically and iron again. The buckram will provide stiffness and hold the creases. You now have your very own custom map!

Amanda Wood loves Helvetica, a good single-origin Earl Grey tea, and constantly reorganizing her things. She finds inspiration in the work of her children and in artists Tilleke Schwarz, Anni Albers, Maira Kalman, and Bruno Munari. In 2012, Amanda began making things in earnest while enrolled in the Textile Arts program at Capilano University in North Vancouver, British Columbia. She enjoys the meditative aspects of embroidery and the satisfaction of creating a beautiful thing out of a piece of string, whether the technique is sewing, surface design, or weaving. *woodtextilestudio.wordpress.com*; *owlandpussycat.etsy.com*

Chapter Seven

FICTIONAL CHARACTERS

There sat the poor miller's daughter, and for the life of her, she could not tell what to do. She had no idea how straw could be spun into gold, and she grew more and more frightened, until at last she began to weep.

—excerpt from *Rumpelstiltskin,* **by the Brothers Grimm**

What if?

Alberto Manguel wrote: "We give the image a before and an after." That's what makes an image a narrative. When something is normal, we don't wonder about it. I like those things that are a bit ambiguous and absurd.

—**artist Bettina Matzkuhn**

Fiction provides us with the opportunity to ask, *What if*? By offering unlimited possibilities, fictional stories let us see beyond our personal experiences and witness events through circumstances that are not our own. Through these stories, we experience the lives of others in their best moments, worst hours, and even on those mundane days that, in retrospect, may seem profound. While we may not share similar histories or life experiences with the fictional characters we encounter, when we experience a story through their voice, we briefly inhabit their values and choices. As readers, we experience their heroism and triumphs, their heartbreaks and setbacks. Their victories become our own.

Textiles have been present in storytelling at least since Ariadne led Theseus out of a labyrinth with a length of thread. The Three Fates in Greek mythology spun yarn and cut it, sealing the destinies of mortals. In literature, the Lady of Shalott was confined with only her loom for company, Cinderella was transformed by a beautiful dress, and Little Red Riding Hood's grandmother was fooled by a red cape.

The artists in this chapter re-create well-known fictional characters from iconic types of storytelling—fairytales, comic folklore, and horror stories. Some, like Mark Newport, challenge the conventions of a well-known story archetype. His work allows us to question what happens when these familiar characters act differently than we expect them to. Artists like Stephanie Dosen and Tracy Widdess create works that celebrate characters from a fantastical realm. Their work allows us to imagine ourselves as fairytale creatures or horrific monsters, as light and fantastical or dark and predatory.

Let the work in this chapter allow you to ponder how fiction affects you and your outlook on the world. How can you incorporate fictional stories into your textile works? Which characters have stayed with you long past the close of a book's cover? What qualities did these characters possess that made them linger in your mind?

FIBER AND FAIRYTALES:

An Interview with Stephanie Dosen of Tiny Owl Knits

Stephanie Dosen lives in the foothills of the Rocky Mountains. A successful singer-songwriter, Stephanie has performed with Virus, Chemical Brothers, and Massive Attack. She also released several solo albums and, in 2009, started a band called Snowbird with Simon Raymonde (former member of Cocteau Twins). She describes her third album, released in 2013, as being "like Snow White and Kira from The Dark Crystal got together to make music in the woods." Stephanie balances her musical career with her ethereal knitting company Tiny Owl Knits. She designs whimsical patterns inspired by fairytale lore. Stephanie released a knitting book based on her company called Woodland Knits in fall 2013. *tinyowlknits.com*

Tiny Owl Knits, *Sleeping Beauty Cowl*, 2011, crochet.
Photo: Stephanie Dosen.

Q: You've created works around Alice in Wonderland, Rapunzel, and Sleeping Beauty—characters revisited by artists many times in books and movies. How do you approach designing when the end project evokes a beloved character?

A: For me, it starts with the design, which almost always comes before the name. I have my own personal fairytale relationship with the pattern before I start thinking about how it relates to a story. At the end of the design process, I look at it and think, "Oh! That's a hat for Rapunzel!"

Q: One of my favorite patterns in your collection is the *Wear the Wild Things Are* jumper and crown, as I've always been a big fan of author Maurice Sendak. Have you heard any unusual stories of Max-like adventures or transformations from those who have made it?

A: I like to see pictures of kids wearing this costume, but I especially love to see pictures of adults! You can see in their eyes that they are suddenly romping in the forest, causing a wild and wonderful ruckus. The sweater and hat give them an excuse to prance around and act like they are having a monster party. It's amazing how clothing gives us "permission" to act in a way we normally wouldn't. I think it makes us all a bit braver. ✳

Clockwise from top left: Tiny Owl Knits, *Alice in Wonderland*, 2009, crochet; *Wear The Wild Things Are*, 2009, knitting;, *Grimm's Cottage Capelet*, 2011, knitting. Photos: Stephanie Dosen

SUPERHERO STORIES:

An Interview with Mark Newport

Mark Newport is an artist and teacher who lives in the suburbs of Detroit, Michigan. His work explores ideas of gender, especially masculinity, through the use of comic-book superheroes. In 1997, he began working with a series of embroidered bedcovers and samplers made of comic-book pages, and in 2003 his work began to include a series of hand-knit, life-sized superhero costumes. Mark has created photographs, prints, videos, and performances while wearing his knitted costumes, and recently he has been carving action figures based on the toys of his youth. His work inspires viewers to consider our idea of superheroes, gender assumptions, and our cultural expectations of how power relates to these perceived ideals. *marknewportartist.com*

Mark Newport, *W Man*, 2009, hand-knit acrylic and buttons, 120 x 28 x 6 in (304.8 x 71.12 x 15.24 cm). Photo: Mark Newport

Q: Your body of work includes knitting and embroidery, both of which have been traditionally considered "feminine" hobbies. How and why did you learn these skills?

A: My grandmother taught me to knit, embroider, and sew when I was a boy. In college, I transferred from painting to fiber, and later I relearned embroidery as a graduate teaching assistant for an embellishment class. I returned to knitting in 2000 when I wanted to add it to a three-dimensional fiber class that I taught.

During my studies, I realized that I work best when I am doing very tactile, repetitive, detailed work like weaving, knitting, and other textile processes. I needed the time and the physical connection that those processes involve in order to help develop my ideas and explore themes in a work. While I was an undergrad, I began making work about gender roles. As a result of my studies, I understood that the social and historical link of textiles to women's work and feminism made them ideal tools for exploration. They provide a contradiction to the hyper-masculine images of heroes.

Q: You are known for your knitted superhero suits. How did you start making them?

A: The costumes were a logical development from my earlier embroidered comic-book works. I was thinking about the concept of protection, as I had small children who were making attempts to gain independence—riding bikes to friends' houses or the park and the like. I could not keep an eye on them, and it worried me. That is natural, but so was their desire for independence. On a larger stage, it was post 9/11 and on the news there was talk about the border, safety, terrorism, and a hypersensitivity regarding self-protection. I started thinking about who protects us and who represents protection. I felt that the image of the superhero was perfect. The first costume was Batman. I used a raglan sweater pattern from the Internet because I wanted to knit it in the round, creating it as much in one piece as possible.

Q: Your artist statement says, "These characters are childhood memories of the ultimate man." Can you elaborate on this?

A: Superheroes were rich and formative symbols when I was young. Each hero has different qualities that represent the ideal characteristics of an adult who is powerful and in control (sometimes)—someone we aspire to be. That type of heroism is ultimately unattainable, and I think our teen and early adult years teach us that. So the symbol stays alive, but more as a memory or a childhood hope inside the adult, who knows he cannot be that person but might still wish to be.

Q: *Real Heroes* are well-known characters from comic-book lore and cowboy movies, but the pieces in the Sweatermen series are heroes of your own invention.

A: The basic difference between the Real Heroes and the Sweatermen is how much I focus on the knitting. For the most part, in *Real Heroes*, the knitting transforms the hero costume from a body-fitting, dynamic symbol to a lumpy, saggy, bulky sweater-like version of Batman or Spiderman. In Sweatermen, the traditions, textures, and design elements of knitting become the focal point of the costume and really push the knitting to the fore. In each case, the knitting is there as a reference to a quiet, domestic, labor-intensive,

Mark Newport, *Batman 3*, 2006, hand-knit acrylic and buttons, 80 x 23 x 6 in (203.2 x 58.42 x 15.24 cm). Photo: Mark Newport

Mark Newport, *Big Ends Man*, 2012, hand-knit acrylic and buttons, 120 x 28 x 6 in (304.8 x 71.12 x 15.24 cm). Photo: Mark Newport

and traditionally feminine way of working that contradicts the impulsive, dynamic, aggressive actions of a superhero. With the invented heroes, I think the knitting becomes the emblem of the hero's power and asks the question, "Can knitting be protective and powerful?"

Q: You have invented heroes with names like *Sweatermen*, *Every-Any-No Man*, and *Bobbleman*. How important is character development in your practice?

A: All of the costumes in Real Heroes and Sweatermen are based in a backstory that I developed. I have a family, and the news tells me that I need to protect them from terrorists, pedophiles, drug dealers, and other dangers in the world. But how do I do that? I have to become a superhero, because they are the people who protect everyone. So I need a costume. I knit it because it can stretch and move as I perform my heroic activities. It takes two months of sitting quietly to make one, and doing so makes me realize that knitting generates my super-power—the ability to make a force field while knitting. Invented heroes allow me to explore the textures and designs traditional to knitting such as cables and bobbles and sweater-types like those made from ends of leftover yarn and the materials that I find.

Q: I understand that you knit the suits to fit your body, but sometimes play with the proportions of the suit.

A: Some of the suits, like *Fantastic Four*, *Every-Any-No-Man*, and the more recent *Big Batman*, *Big Ends Man*, and *Big S Man 1* and *2*, are obviously not going to fit me. These costumes are eight to ten feet [2.43 to 3.05 m] tall. It started with the Fantastic Four costume, as that character's superpower is to be able to stretch to any size. I was interested in what happens to the costume and the body as his power acts up and he cannot return to his normal size. The more recent Big Hero series builds off the scale relationship that costume has to the viewer—like parent to child or rescuer to rescued.

In *Bobbleman*, I extended the length of the legs because I had realized that, in the other pieces, my proportions do not meet the heroic, sculptural ideals. I could lengthen the legs and become more like that ideal. In *Batman 3*, I based the proportions of the costume on an action figure of Batman as a middle-aged, bulky man and then scaled up the figure's measurements for a six-foot [1.83-m] tall man. It was an exploration of the bodily image of the hero and how that relates to average human bodies.

Q: Some of the suits focus on knitting techniques—bobbles, cables, and knitted pattern. Why did you choose to focus on knitting technique as the strongest visual element?

A: Knitting has associations with the feminine, home, domesticity, patience, peacefulness—all qualities that contradict traditional associations of the superhero. By highlighting the knitting, I want to make that contradiction more evident and ask questions about how we represent power. The knitted elements become the hero's emblem and represent his superpower.

Q: With the Freedom Bedcovers, you've combined comic-book pages and embroidery into a quilt. Is the comic meant to be read on the quilt or have you changed the story in the way that you've put it together?

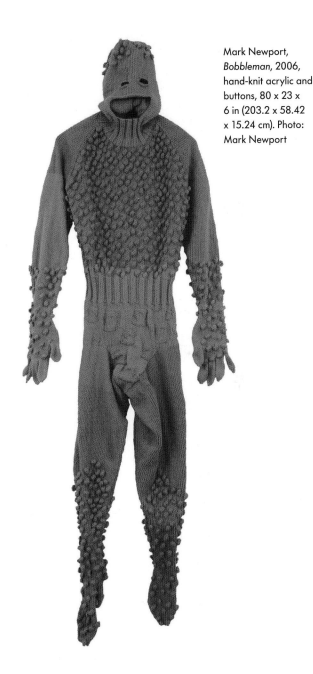

Mark Newport, *Bobbleman*, 2006, hand-knit acrylic and buttons, 80 x 23 x 6 in (203.2 x 58.42 x 15.24 cm). Photo: Mark Newport

Mark Newport, *Freedom Bedcover: Zachary*, 2006, embroidery on comic book pages, 85 x 65 in (215 x 165.1 cm). Photo: Mark Newport

A: The use of comic-book pages grew from earlier work I did that involved transforming trading cards by sewing beads over the images on the cards. Comic books seemed like a logical extension of that process, and the bedcovers originated in test embroidering on the pages. While doing these tests, a friend told me about *Freedom Quilts*. These quilts were given to a young man upon leaving his father's home, usually on his twenty-first birthday. I was interested in the history of those quilts and their symbolic functions: protection, connection, independence, and adulthood. Those are not things that I saw honored in my transition into adulthood. I decided to use the comic-book pages because the heroes on them could be seen as role models for what an adult could be, and as talismans for protection. The bedcovers explore that transition to adulthood in a form that cannot protect or connect the user to others in a truly meaningful way.

The pages in each bedcover come from several different comic books so the stories in the originals are lost. The narrative of the pieces comes from the heroes and what they mean for the viewer. ✳

Mark Newport, detail of *Freedom Bedcover: Zachary*. Photo: Mark Newport

Prompt

Fictional Characters

Bring fiction into your own textile artwork. You can imagine and invent a character or put your own spin on a character that we all know and love.

If working with an established character like Sherlock Holmes or Pippi Longstocking, ask yourself the following questions to prompt new ideas:

1. What do they look like?

2. What elements can be conjured from memory and what needs to be researched?

3. What do they sound like?

4. What is an aspect of their character that is not widely known? How can you enhance this with your design?

5. What is his or her attitude about life? What is their mood when they wake up in the morning? Can this be captured in a facial expression?

6. How might this character be misunderstood?

If you are creating a new character, ask yourself the following questions to evoke a well-rounded presence:

1. What is their temperament?

2. What do they look like?

3. What is their favorite thing to do?

4. What are they most scared of?

5. What is their best quality?

6. What materials and colors best show off their personality?

KNITTING NIGHTMARES:
An Interview with Tracy Widdess

Tracy Widdess has received international acclaim for her knitted monsters and her art practice, Brutal Knitting. A self-taught knitter who picked up her needles in response to a former roommate's twee creations, Tracy has become a technically astute sculptor of knitted brutes, monsters, and specters. Nightmarish, comical, odd, and wildly appealing in its grotesqueness, Tracy's knitting can cause spectacular nightmares complete with wooly horns, scales, warts, and tentacles. She lives in Port Alberni, British Columbia.

Tracy Widdess, *Why Be Yourself When You Can Be A Decorative Ulcer*, 2012, yarn, glass beads, 20 x 15 x 15 in (50.8 x 38.1 x 38.1 cm). Photo: Tracy Widdess

Q: How did Brutal Knitting start?

A: When I first started knitting in 1999, I knew that I wanted to focus on something bigger. I ended up being connected with a charity project in which people were knitting mask patterns from the 1970s. I saw some masks in *Threads* magazine in a 1992 article by Meg Swanson called "Snow Fooling," and I said I'd make one because I couldn't believe they were in a magazine—they were unbelievably strange. April Winchell, who was running the project, ended up featuring me on Regretsy, and my knitting got a lot of attention for it. It gave me a direction for Brutal Knitting.

The pieces are hand and machine knit. I stay up all night with my knitting machines. Once I started to get commissions, I was able to buy two. I thought they would alleviate my workload because they can create a great deal of knitted yardage, but they made my work more complex. There are a lot of pre-conceived notions of what knitting machines can do, but really, they just create more problems. You still have to bind it off. You have to rethread all of the loops onto a US 0/2 mm needle. It was a rude awakening for me, but I like a challenge—it keeps me interested. And I like the way the fabric looks too. I don't have anything against crochet, I just like the complexity of knitting and the flat way that knit fabric looks.

When I was a student, I took a sculpture class, and I couldn't do the first project. Making something three-dimensional for the first time was incredibly hard. That's why I focused on it with my knitting, because I couldn't do it in art school. I like the challenge. I briefly had a roommate who knitted pretty hats and scarves for her friends, and I thought, How come you can knit and I can't? I had to teach myself

Tracy Widdess, *The Night Crawler*, 2011, yarn, 11 x 15 in (27.9 x 38.1 cm).
Photo: Tracy Widdess

to knit out of spite. Thirteen years later, I realize that I'm getting to be one of the best people at doing this—which is pretty fun, considering I started completely self-taught from books at the library.

Q: Your body of work consists of masks of well-known monsters and fictional characters. What is your design process?

A: I usually have a lot of leeway in terms of keeping the characters recognizable or not. The fictional characters are straight out of my head. I usually make them in the periods between my commissioned projects. A lot of times, I end up making something that doesn't work. Sometimes I mash a bunch of things together that are pieces of a failed bunch of other things, and the end result becomes something better. I never pre-plan or draw something out, as I've already done the design work in my head. I sculpt everything over a fake head. I try not to spend three weeks on something, but generally I work between fifty and 100 hours on each mask.

Q: How do you research your well-known characters? It must feel like a big responsibility to create a knitted version of a character that most of us know.

A: I'm so hungry for images that searching for them is how I relax. I use eBay and Flickr a lot for finding images. When I was researching Krampus, I saved everything I found. It is embarrassing; I've probably collected between twenty and forty images a day for the past four years.

I get a general sense of what the character looks like, and I make my own version out of the parts that seem the most appealing. In *Gruß von Krampus*, my main goal was to create the spiraled horns. How do you knit a spiral horn? I had to figure it out. I have no problem going in and editing my work; I change it. I couldn't care less what happens with it. Someone could put it in the compost bin; it goes out the door as fast as it can.

Q: What sort of feedback have you had about your work?

A: A lot of people say that they haven't seen anything like it. My work was in a music video for a Waters song called "For the One." I find that having my work in film and television is really appealing. I hope to do more commissions in this field because I like my work being part of a larger story.

I hope that people see the humor in what I do. It is not serious. A lot of people don't think that [the pieces] are funny, but they are supposed to be funny. ✳

Tracy Widdess, *Gruß vom Krampus*, 2011, yarn, glass beads, 17 x 11 x 11 in (43.18 x 27.9 x 27.9 cm). Photo: Tracy Widdess

Tracy Widdess, *Monetize Mint*, 2012, yarn, 27 x 11 x 11 in (68.58 x 27.9 x 27.9 cm). Photo: Tracy Widdess

Left: Tracy Widdess, *Haus zum Walfisch*, 2013, yarn, 20 x 15 x 15 in (50.8 x 38.1 x 38.1 cm). Photo: Tracy Widdess

Right: Tracy Widdess, *Jabberwocky*, 2011, yarn, 25 x 15 x 15 in (63.5 x 38.1 x 38.1 cm). Photo: Tracy Widdess

Project

The Amelia Mobile

SUSAN KENDAL

Facts and fancy about Amelia Earhart inspired each of the pieces on Susan Kendal's mobile of soft-sculpture items made of felt. The Amelia Mobile can be hung as a mobile for an infant or as an art object for anyone to enjoy.

Creating a Narrative from Amelia's Life

In making the Amelia Mobile, Susan read and wondered about Amelia Earhart's life. She came up with some objects that she thought represented her real and imaginary biography: the red nose and steel propeller of the Lockheed Vega in which Amelia crossed the Atlantic on her historic solo flight; the nuts and bolts so vital to planes, which she incorporated as buttons in her fashion line; a paper airplane; a freckle-cream jar, recently discovered on a remote island in the Pacific where scientists and historians think Amelia might have crashed and survived for a time; a compass modeled on one from the 1930s; a re-creation of Amelia's fashion-line label; an aviation hat and goggles modeled on a set that Amelia wore early in her career; and a pilot's pin. When it came time to craft, Susan needed to make these objects a similar size so that the mobile would be balanced.

The Amelia Mobile can be modified or personalized; you can let your imagination and research run wild. Make a mobile of someone else famous or not-so-famous—or even someone fictitious—someone who inspires you. Look for eight obvious and not so obvious objects that represent the individual's life. Susan chose a white inverted umbrella for a mobile hanging system because it provides a ready-made frame and a beautiful canvas of cloudy sky, but you can be creative here too—use an oven rack, a tree branch, or an embroidery ring. While Amelia Earhart is far from a fictional character, this kind of project frees you to imagine the possibilities of what her life might have been like—the sky's the limit (pun intended).

TOOLS & MATERIALS

- paper suitable for a desktop printer
- scissors (small and very sharp)
- straight pins
- tailor's chalk
- size 4 or 5 embroidery needle
- sewing machine
- sewing thread in brown, black, and off-white (for machine and hand finishing)
- Marlow Whipping Twine, size 2, waxed, for hanging the mobile pieces. Other brands of strong twine or dental floss can be substituted.
- embroidery floss: 1 skein each of:
  - DMC White
  - DMC 321 Red
  - DMC 976 Md Golden Brown
  - DMC 301 Black
  - DMC 3799 Vy Dk Pewter Grey
  - DMC 898 Dk Coffee Brown
- 12 sheets felt (Susan used a wool/rayon blend, purchased from Sweet Emma Jean on Etsy.), 1 each of:

• Antique White	• Reets Relish
• Aged Bronze	• Strawberry Parfait
• Black	• Safari Brown
• Blue Spruce	• Silver Grey
• Mustard Relish	• Smokey Marble
• Peat Moss	• Straw

- 1 lb (500 g) wool or poly batting for stuffing
- white umbrella (16-rib Doorman umbrella, shown in photographs)
- 1 large cup hook

SKILLS

- basic operation of a sewing machine
- intermediate sewing
- intermediate embroidery (backstitch, blanket stitch, running stitch, single detached chain stitch, stem stitch, French knot, whip stitch)

☞ Propeller (figure 1)

FELT COLORS: Strawberry Parfait, Black, Smokey Marble
EMBROIDERY FLOSS COLORS: Red, Black, Pewter Grey

....

Cut one piece each of A (Black), B (Strawberry Parfait), C (Black), and E (Smokey Marble). Cut four D pieces (Smokey Marble).

Create the plane's nose:
Place A over B so that it overlaps by 0.25 in (6 mm) and machine-stitch it onto A using a tight, wide zigzag stitch.

Using a running stitch and 2 strands of red floss, stitch around perimeter of red B piece, 0.25 in (6 mm) from the edge. Cinch it by pulling floss tight, making it curl over the A piece.

Roll a modest amount of batting into a long piece and tuck it in, around, and under cinched B piece to create the bulbous nose of the plane. Use a whipstitch and 2 strands of red floss to tack A piece onto B piece once it has been lightly stuffed.

Place C piece in the center of the plane's nose, just covering red cinching of B piece. Whipstitch C onto B using black floss.

Using long, single chain stitches and Pewter Grey floss, stitch from center of piece C to the North, South, East, and West, securing chain stitches where A and C (red and black, respectively) meet. In between stitches, make 4 more single chain stitches to secure them on piece C, 0.25 in (6 mm) in from piece B (red).

Create the propeller:

Stack 2 D pieces on top of one another, right sides facing, and machine stitch them together with a 0.25-in (6-mm) seam allowance. Repeat with other 2 D pieces. Notch curve and trim seam down to 0.125 in (3 mm), then turn the propeller blades right-side out.

Using a running stitch and 2 threads of Pewter Grey floss, top stitch propeller blades 0.25 in (6 mm) from edge so they lie flat.

Fold open ends of propeller blades in half and tack them in place making a single pleat. Stitch them together, 1 pleat up, 1 pleat down, so it looks like the blades are slightly twisted.

Wrap E piece around attached propeller blades and whipstitch to close using Pewter Grey floss. Stitch into the propeller blades. Tack connected and wrapped propeller securely into center of C.

☞ Aviator hat and goggles (figure 2)

FELT COLORS: Safari Brown, Peat Moss, Silver Grey, Straw
EMBROIDERY FLOSS COLOR: Pewter Grey, Brown, Black

. . . .

Cut 1 piece each of A, B, and C (all in Safari Brown), and F (Straw). Cut 4 pieces each of D (Peat Moss) and 2 pieces of E (Silver Grey).

Create hat:

Machine stitch A to one side of C, right sides facing, with 0.25-in (6-mm) seam allowance. Notch curves and clip seams down to 0.125 in (3 mm), then turn right-side out, massaging seams into curve of hat. Repeat for B onto the other side of C.

Create goggles:

Stack an E piece on top of a D piece and stitch around E piece to secure using a small running stitch and 2 strands of Pewter Grey.

Place another D piece against back of stitched D/E piece, and attach it using blanket stitch with Coffee Brown floss.

Repeat for other goggle.

Using 2 strands of black floss, stitch between 2 D/E goggle pieces where nosepiece attaches (marked with an asterisk on D pattern pieces), then wrap stitches with blanket stitch.

Whipstitch ends of piece F, goggle strap, onto back of D/E goggle pieces, with 0.5 in (1 cm) seam allowance on which to sew goggle strap.

Place goggles on hat and stitch them in place using brown sewing thread. The strap can sit around the hat.

☞ Nuts and bolt (figure 3)

FELT COLOR: Silver Grey
EMBROIDERY FLOSS COLOR: Pewter Grey

. . . .

Cut 8 pieces of A and 1 each of B and C (all in Silver Grey).

Create nuts:

Stack 4 A pieces on top of one another, lining up the 8 sides. Use a running stitch and 2 strands Pewter Grey floss to stitch together. Stitch around central circle and then around octagon's edges.

Repeat for second nut.

Create bolt:

For bolt head, use a running stitch and 2 strands of Pewter

Grey floss to stitch around edges of the B piece, 0.125 in (3 mm) from edge. Pull stitches to cinch the circle. Before closing bolt head, roll a small piece of batting in your hands and stuff it into bolt head. Cinch circle tightly around the batting to create bolt head. Before tying off thread, sew 2 running stitches through top of bolt to create cross, "X."

For bolt's long body, roll C piece tightly. Using 2 strands Pewter Grey, blanket stitch open side to close. Wrap floss in a spiral down the bolt's body to create the "threading" of a bolt.

Stitch to bolt head using cinched excess as an attachment point.

Carefully clip end of bolt body to create a point at tip.

☞ Amelia Earhart fashion label (figure 4)

FELT COLOR: Straw

EMBROIDERY FLOSS COLORS: Black, Red

....

Cut two pieces of A (Straw).

On one of A pieces, outline Amelia Earhart's signature using tailor's chalk. You can freehand it onto your felt, using pattern piece provided or do an Internet search for "Amelia Earhart fashion label" to see a photo of an original label.

Using a tiny backstitch and 2 strands of black floss, stitch along signature. Use a French knot for the dot on the i.

Outline the red plane and its diagonal flight path with tailor's chalk.

Using a tiny backstitch and 1 strand of red floss, sew along flight path and stitch the plane.

Using stem stitch and all 6 strands of black embroidery thread, outline entire A piece 0.125 in (3 mm) from edge of label.

Pin second A piece against back of embroidered piece and, using a whipstitch and off-white sewing thread, stitch together. Pass stitches through back of black stem stitches that outline the label. Label should now be cleanly backed.

☞ Paper airplane (figure 5)

FELT COLOR: Straw

EMBROIDERY FLOSS COLOR: White

....

Cut 1 piece of A (Straw).

Fold corner to corner to form a triangle.

Using a running stitch and 2 strands of white floss, stitch the 2 open sides of triangle together.

Fold corner to corner again to form a smaller triangle.

Using a running stitch again, sew fold. Stitch as close to the fold as you can, 0.125–0.25 in (3–6 mm) from fold.

Fold 1 open corner down so that its flat side sits parallel to the central "spine" fold you've just stitched. The point now protrudes beyond back of plane. Sew along this fold as you did on spine of plane. This will keep wing folded.

Repeat on other side.

Now you're ready to fly away!

☞ Compass (figure 6)

FELT COLORS: Blue Spruce, Peat Moss

EMBROIDERY FLOSS COLOR: Black, Golden Brown

....

Cut 2 pieces each of A (Blue Spruce) and B (Peat Moss). Cut 1 C piece (Peat Moss).

Using blanket stitch and 2 strands of Golden Brown floss, attach 2 B pieces on inside seam of circle.

Use same stitch and floss to stitch edge of entire C piece, the dial.

Attach C piece to center of one of the A pieces using a French knot and 2 strands of Golden Brown floss.

Stitch capital letters N, E, S, and W onto working piece A at their appropriate direction points. Use small backstitches and French knots on ends of letters with black floss.

Turn compass dial (C) to direction at which you would like to secure it and stitch a small circle around French knot using small backstitches in 2 strands of black floss.

Stack unused A piece against back of the embroidered A piece and place B frame piece over it. Secure all 4 pieces with blanket stitch using 2 strands of black floss.

Make a couple of over-and-over stitches at the 4 compass points and add a French knot to each point.

☞ Freckle cream jar (figure 7)

FELT COLORS: Antique White, Straw, Reets Relish, Mustard Relish
EMBROIDERY FLOSS COLOR: Golden Brown, White

....

Cut 2 pieces each of A (Antique White), C and D (Reets Relish), and E (Mustard Relish) and 1 each of B and F (Antique White) and G (Straw).

Create jar:
Machine or hand sew B to 1 of the A pieces following the lines of A piece, right sides facing. This is fussy, so it may prove easiest to do by hand, with a 0.25-in (6-mm) seam allowance. Repeat with second A piece to create the felt jar. Notch corners and curves and cut seam down to 0.125 in (3 mm), then turn jar right-side out.

Generously stuff jar with wool or poly batting to create jar shape with stuffing.

Machine or hand stitch F piece ends together to create circle with 0.25-in (6-mm) seam allowance.

Use the F piece circle to line the inside lip of jar with seams facing each other. Blanket stitch F to lip of jar using 2 strands of white floss.

Tuck G piece into finished opening of jar to cover the batting. Position it at the lower inside edge of the jar lip so jar looks full of cream. Secure with a few invisible running stitches to F piece using off-white sewing thread.

Create label:
Using a running stitch and Golden Brown floss, attach E pieces onto centers of C pieces.

On 1 of the E pieces, embroider the word "Freckle," using tiny back stitches and 2 strands of Golden Brown floss.

Machine stitch straight sides of C pieces to shorter sides of D pieces to form label, with 0.125-in (3-mm) seam allowance.

Slide label up over jar and align 4 side seams. Secure top and bottom edges of centered label to jar using whip stitch and 2 strands of white floss.

☛ Pilot's wings (figure 8)

FELT COLOR: Aged Bronze

EMBROIDERY FLOSS COLOR: Golden Brown

....

Cut 2 pieces each of A and C and 1 each of B, D, and E (all in Aged Bronze). For pieces A and B, the wings, need to be cut on the fold.

Embroider a central motif onto 1 of the C pieces. Insignias

on pilot's wings often incorporate stars or crowns. This set features an "A" for Amelia. To make the "A," use stem stitch and 2 strands of Golden Bronze floss for the 3 bars and 2 over-and-over stitches on top of each other on the point and ends of the "A" to finish it off with style.

Stack D piece on unused C piece, and E on top of D (D and E are the stuffing). Top with embroidered C piece, making a felt sandwich. Attach C pieces together with blanket stitch. This creates the raised central insignia of the pilot's wings.

Attach B to 1 of the A pieces. Use a running stitch, with a stitch in each "feather" curve and around the top of both wings.

Sew circle insignia onto wings with a running stitch through the back and wings.

Attach second A piece to back of wings with blanket stitch through both A pieces (so that the blanket stitch shows only on back of wings). This gives a clean back to the wings and covers the work of attaching the wings and circle insignia.

☞ Attach Mobile Pieces to Umbrella

Once all your mobile objects are completed, prepare whipping twine and an embroidery needle.

Choose 8 anchor points on umbrella for mobile objects (the ribs will be the strongest areas). Mark points with tailor's chalk or a high-contrast baste stitch.

Find a balance point in each mobile object for hanging. For instance, the wing seam of the paper airplane, rather than its spine, is used as the hanging point so that the plane hangs slightly sideways as if banking through the sky.

Cut a long piece (24–25 in [60–90 cm]) of whipping twine. Make a large knot in the end of the twine and stitch it through

the hanging point. Tug on the knot to make sure it's secure. Tie a knot at the exit point of whipping twine so that object is securely held on twine and won't slide up and down the strand.

For nuts and bolt: All 3 pieces get threaded onto 1 piece of twine. After knotting the first item, make a new knot about 1 in (2.5 cm) up from the item and thread the next one. Repeat for the third item.

Stitch length of twine with mobile object attached to it through the umbrella fabric around one of the ribs. Check that the length is to your liking, then knot thread over rib to secure. Make a few more stitches around the umbrella rib for security, knot, and clip off excess twine.

☛ Display Mobile

The 16-rib Doorman umbrella used in the example is definitely large! Such vast white space relative to the size of the mobile objects makes them appear sparsely scattered across their canvas of sky. The umbrella's handle can be hung over a cup hook placed in the ceiling, or over a beam or cord. The large scope of this mobile means it can look magical over an infant's crib and equally interesting in a space such as a two-story room. Be creative with displaying the mobile, and enjoy your piece of mysterious, Amelia Earhart-laden sky.

Designer **Susan Kendal** is an Ontario-based artist who often works as Pocket Alchemy, her company's moniker. Pocket Alchemy is a vehicle for Susan's creative adventures in textiles and contemporary dance. A lifelong crafter and textile artist, Susan sews beautiful, freehand quilted items for babies and knits things both flat and three-dimensional. She recently fell in love with felt soft sculpture and this is increasingly the focus of her artistic practice. Susan choreographs, teaches, and designs costumes for contemporary dancers and companies in Ontario. She is a graduate of the School of Toronto Dance Theatre's prestigious Professional Training Program in contemporary dance. Susan has two little boys who make motherhood and life a creative, inventive, improvisational journey at every turn. *pocketalchemy.ca*

Propeller

Enlarge at 125%

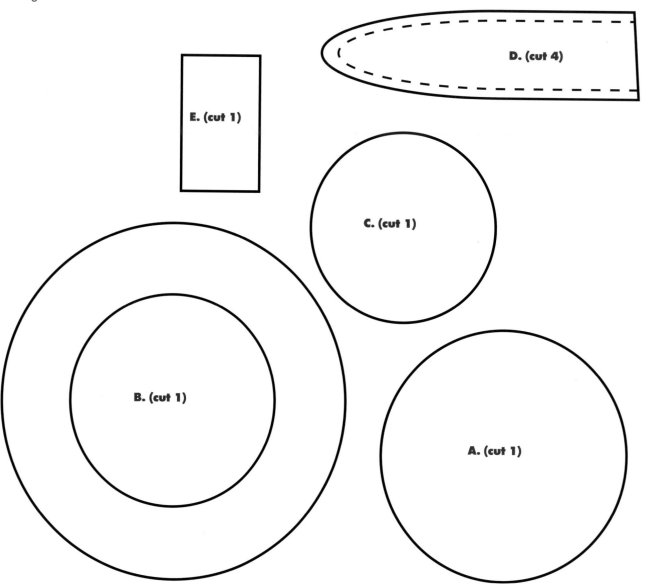

D. (cut 4)

E. (cut 1)

C. (cut 1)

B. (cut 1)

A. (cut 1)

Aviator Hat and Goggles

Enlarge at 125%

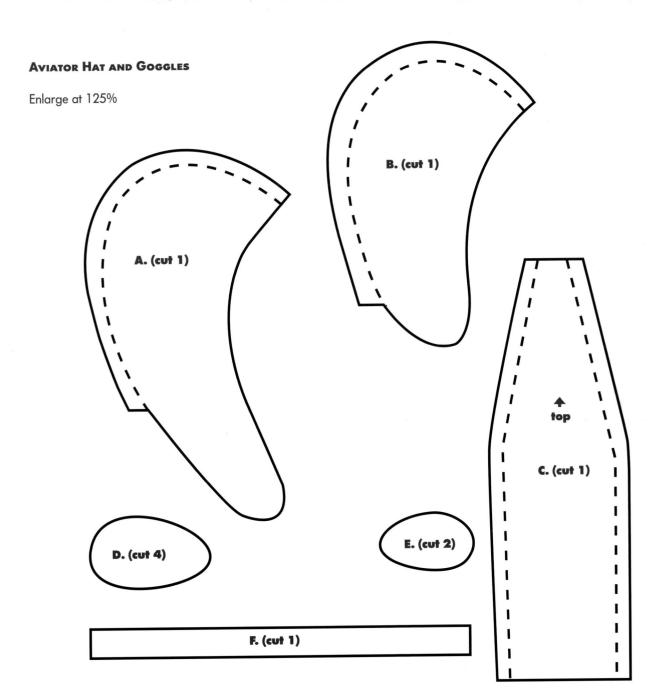

A. (cut 1)

B. (cut 1)

C. (cut 1)

top

D. (cut 4)

E. (cut 2)

F. (cut 1)

Nuts & Bolt

Copy at 100%

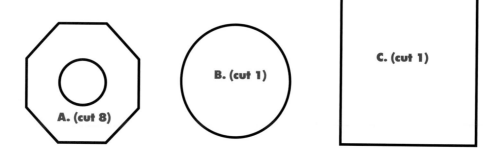

A. (cut 8)

B. (cut 1)

C. (cut 1)

Fashion Label

Copy at 100%

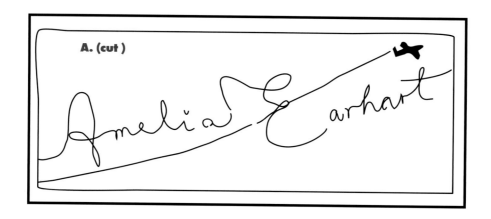

A. (cut)

PAPER AIRPLANE

Copy at 100%

A. (cut 1)

COMPASS

Copy at 100%

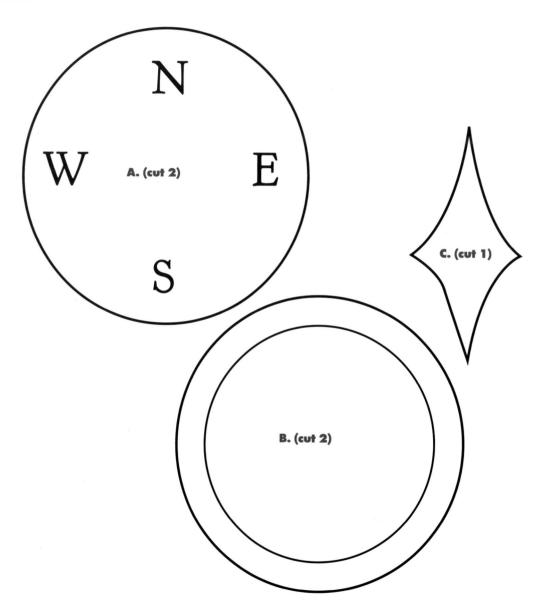

A. (cut 2)

N
W E
S

C. (cut 1)

B. (cut 2)

FRECKLE CREAM JAR

Enlarge at 125%

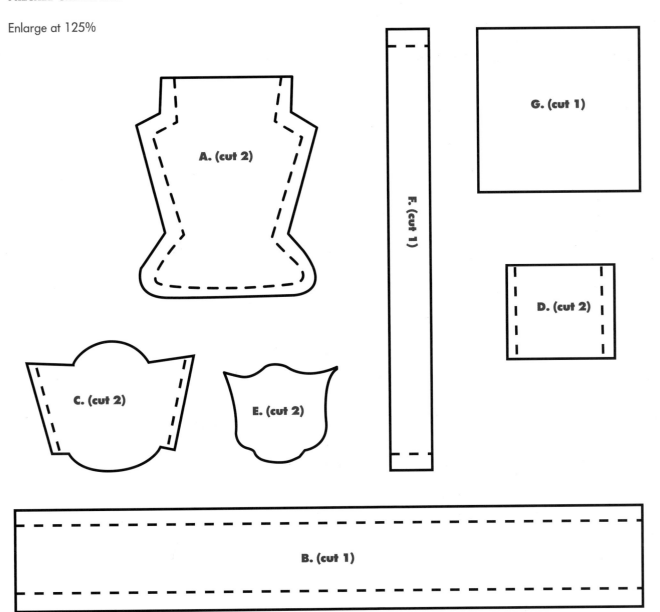

PILOT'S WINGS

Copy at 100%

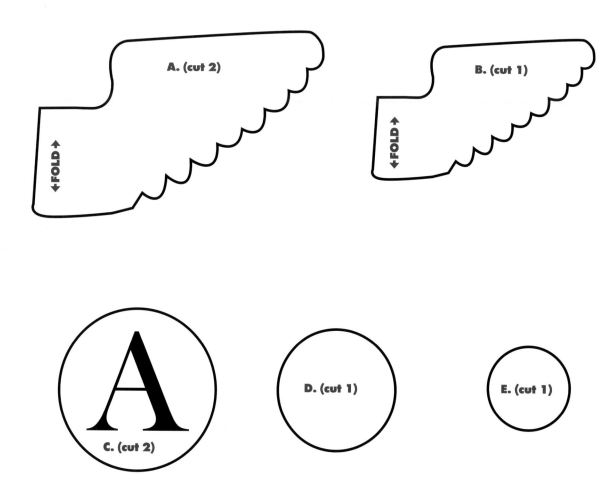

A. (cut 2)

◀FOLD➤

B. (cut 1)

◀FOLD➤

C. (cut 2)

D. (cut 1)

E. (cut 1)

Chapter Eight

HUMOROUS TEXTILES

When I was buying Velcro, the clerk asked what I was going to make. I said, "I'm gonna make a human Mr. Potato Head Mask."

—artist Howie Woo on developing his *Invisibility Mask Project*

Comedy

> *My work mocks issues with playfulness; humor is a great way*
> *to heighten the impact of serious issues.*
>
> *—artist Kirsty Whitlock*

Not all stories are serious. No matter where we come from or what language we speak, we all appreciate a laugh. Whether understated and wry or sidesplitting and guffaw-worthy, comedy is a language developed between people based on observations about our society, culture, and lives. Comedy also has purpose—it can simply tickle the funny bone, or it can break down barriers to make it easier to discuss challenging subjects. Parody, slapstick, irony, or satire are all potent ways to tell a story, whether eyebrows are raised or tears of hilarity ensue.

Handicraft techniques have traditionally been employed in "serious" objects such as wedding quilts, baby knits, or samplers. In contemporary pieces, textiles are often used not to celebrate important life events but to commemorate the ordinary: Internet memes, quotes from flash-in-the-pan celebrities, and YouTube sensations are purposefully captured in embroidery, cross-stitch, felting, and weaving. Seen through the window of popular culture, these icons, once rendered by the hands of a crafter, seem even more ridiculous. From Subversive Cross Stitching's cranky samplers stitched with statements such as, "Fuck Off, I'm Reading," and "You Are Doing It Wrong," to Tracy Widdess's Grumpy Cat knits, there's humor in considering human behaviors through the mediums of fiber craft.

Humor can also arise when textiles are employed in a way that they're "not supposed" to be. A satin-stitched profanity embellishing a doily can elicit a laugh because it contravenes our beliefs about what should and shouldn't be made with fiber. We expect embroidered flowers; we do not expect embroidered swear words. It is the element of surprise, of the unexpected, that elicits a laugh.

The artists profiled in this chapter bring a sense of self-deprecating humor to their work. The wit in these pieces may result from the commemoration of such uncomfortable but universal human experiences as rejection, loss, unemployment, and envy. There's a moment of hilarity that arises from the audacity of the act—how dare someone memorialize trying times in stitchwork? Who needs to see the ephemera of everyday life carefully replicated in embroidery? Such questions may arise but ultimately lead one to smile and say, "I wish that I had thought of that."

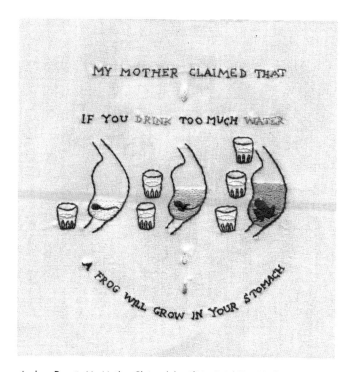

Andrea Dezsö, *My Mother Claimed that If You Drink Too Much Water, A Frog Will Grow in Your Stomach*, 2006, cotton and metallic floss embroidery on cotton fabric, 5 x 5 in (12.7 x 12.7 cm). Photo: Andrea Dezsö

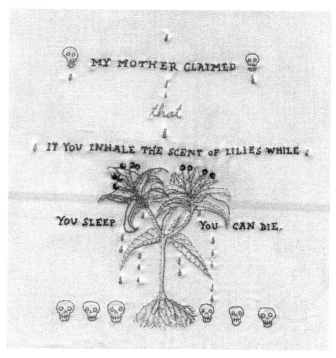

Andrea Dezsö, *My Mother Claimed that Hepatitis is a Liver Disease that You Get From Eating Food You Find Disgusting*, 2006, cotton and metallic floss embroidery on cotton fabric, 5 x 5 in (12.7 x 12.7 cm). Photo: Andrea Dezsö

Andrea Dezsö: Embroidering Ugly "Truths"

Romanian-born and Brooklyn-based artist Andrea Dezsö's Lessons from My Mother consists of forty-eight individually framed cotton squares embroidered with illustrated bits of off-the-wall lies and superstitions told to her by her mother.

Andrea Dezsö, *My Mother Claimed that If You Inhale the Scent of White Lilies While You Sleep, You Can Die*, 2006, cotton and metallic floss embroidery on cotton fabric, 5 x 5 in (12.7 x 12.7 cm). Photo: Andrea Dezsö

Andrea Dezsö, *My Mother Claimed that Men Have Stinky Feet*, 2006, cotton and metallic floss embroidery on cotton fabric, 5 x 5 in (12.7 x 12.7 cm). Photo: Andrea Dezsö

EMBROIDERING A YEAR OF UNEMPLOYMENT:

An Interview with Melissa A. Calderòn

Melissa A. Calderòn describes herself as a "Puerto Rican Bronx girl, born and raised." She is a full-time artist who spends every day in her studio across the street from the Bronx Museum creating multimedia pieces. During a stint of unemployment, she sought relief in the creation of a series of embroidered works that reflected her experience of seeking work and the changes that accompanied this challenging time in her life. The My Unemployed Life series took over a year to complete; Maria stitched six to nine hours every day. There are a total of 90,000 stitches in the project.

Melissa A. Calderòn, *Control* from the *My Unemployed Life* series, 2011, satin and cotton embroidery on linen, 11 x 14 in (27.94 x 35.56 cm). Photo: Melissa A. Calderòn

Q: Tell me about the My Unemployed Life series.

A: Faced with a lack of steady employment in 2010, I decided to take up a needle, channel my grandmother, and make work about the life I was living as an unemployed artist. With no money but plenty of time on my hands, the pieces I called *Control, Luck, Benefit*, and *Prone* came to life. It took over a year to make those four embroideries.

I describe my work as a bricolage of mediums—tissues, steel, gold, and threads—all held together with an ideological glue. Working with different mediums is a part of my process, and I couldn't imagine working any other way.

Q: Is it autobiographical?

A: All of my work is autobiographical. Each work comes from a contemplative time in my life during which large decisions about my life path came into question. Motherhood, cultural identity, loss, self-reliance—the work I make reflects the milestones that each of us go through. We all come to many forks in the road, and that's what I hope to make work about; the indeterminacy and potential of the artist's "road less traveled."

Q: What inspired the four pieces in this series?

A: Each embroidery in the series came from a state of mind I went through during that year. *Control* was my realization that changes interfere with life, and there is nothing to be done about it but keep moving forward. *Benefit* began with the realization that things were hard everywhere and that help was hard to find and difficult to receive. *Prone* was the utter doubt and defeatist attitude I had when nothing was going right—my worn green couch and dog were a comfort to me, away from harsh reality. Finally, *Luck* was the chance I was taking on myself, hoping that something could and would come along that was better than anything I could imagine. Each piece represents a part of the process and illustrates a milestone crossed during a difficult journey.

Q: Is embroidery a good storytelling medium?

A: Embroidery is one of the oldest storytelling mediums. It's a women's traditional medium, which is historically both aristocratic enough for leisure and common enough for labor. I embroidered the last hankie my grandmother ever used with her initials, and I find there is nothing stronger and more permanent than the power of the stitch.

Q: Humor plays into your work. Do you consciously employ it?

A: I feel that humor has a definite place in my work, and whenever I can, I enjoy using it. Sometimes I work with difficult subjects, and I find that adding some fun can also add a level of understanding that might not resonate without it.

Q: Did creating this series change your feelings about a year of unemployment?

A: I tried to make the best of my situation and, like any artist, put that energy into creating work. Each piece of art is work, and I call it "work" because the creative process is a job that an artist has to be present for each day, like any

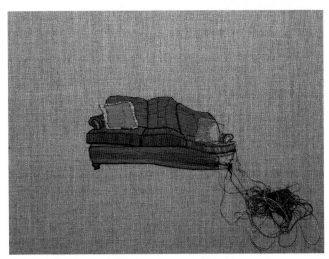

Top: Melissa A. Calderòn, *Benefit* from the *My Unemployed Life* series, 2011, satin and cotton embroidery on linen, 11 x 14 in (27.94 x 35.56 cm). Photo: Melissa A. Calderòn

Bottom: Melissa A. Calderòn, *Prone* from the *My Unemployed Life* series, 2011, satin and cotton embroidery on linen, 11 x 14 in (27.94 x 35.56 cm). Photo: Melissa A. Calderòn

Melissa A. Calderòn, *Luck* from the *My Unemployed Life* series, 2011, satin and cotton embroidery on linen, 11 x 14 in (27.94 x 35.56 cm). Photo: Melissa A. Calderòn

IN THE 1970S,

slogan T-shirts declared, "I'm with Stupid," "Kiss Me I'm Irish," or "Baby on Board." Instant billboards for the human body, the slogan T-shirt has remained an icon of wearable humor, from punny shirts to sophisticated visual oddities of art available through online stores such as *threadless.com.*

other job. It is rewarding and challenging. I feel that year gave me courage and perspective, and without it I may never have gotten to the place I am today.

Q: Your website describes these works as "lovingly" embroidered and notes that this series "converted a difficult, fallow time of unemployment into a starting place for beauty and thoughtfulness."

A: This was a time of loss for me as well as others who were affected by the financial crisis. I experienced a loss of work, loss of my apartment, loss of the neighborhood where I had grown up. It wasn't an easy time, but working every day on those embroideries really got me through while I searched for a job and tried to make ends meet. I had no choice but to hibernate and save, so I took a skill that my grandmother had taught me and made work that reflected my situation. Embroidery is a deeply meditative process and through it, I was able to find peace and personal progress in my life and in my art.

Q: Embroidery can be considered a sentimental medium, but unemployment is a state that most people are unsentimental about. Your work commemorates a time in your life that most people would choose to forget.

A: It's the job of the artist to speak about what they see and experience and interpret it through their palette. Every part of creating a new work is a journey in itself, and I chose to document it the way I know best, through my work. ✻

WOOWORK:

An Interview with Howie Woo

Based in Coquitlam, British Columbia, Howie Woo is an artist of many talents: animation, filmmaking, illustration, comics, storyboarding, writing and, of course, crochet. At *WooWork.com*, he posts his original multi-media stories of the adventures of his own crocheted amigurumi characters: mushroom people, "cuteapillers," robots, and his self-reflexive characters Woomi and Old Man Woo. Whether telling a micro-story through a photograph of a yarn creation or creating a complex tale about jetting off into space on a secret mission, Howie's art is clever, thoughtful, and always bound to make you giggle. *WooWork.com*

Howie Woo and his crocheted alter-ego Woomi, 2008, yarn and fiber filling, 14 x 4 in (35.56 x 10.16 cm). Photo: MJ Kuhn

Q: Tell me about yourself.

A: I've always described myself as a storyteller. I use all the artsy tools that I know or take the time to learn to help tell those stories. When I was growing up, my dad liked to tell stories at the dinner table. He was gregarious, much like my girlfriend MJ is. But I always preferred to tell stories in a more controlled fashion. In person, I'm not a great storyteller. I tend to be too self-conscious. But the impulse to share stories has always been there, and I used drawings and moving images to do that. I never predicted that crochet would become one of those storytelling elements.

Q: Some of your images are visual micro-fictions.

A: I like images that suggest being dropped into the middle of a story and letting our imaginations fill in the rest.

Q: How did learning to crochet change your approach to storytelling?

A: Before crochet, I spent a lot of time drawing for a science magazine. I drew digitally and emailed the files to them. Weeks later, I'd see them printed. What struck me most about making amigurumi was the three-dimensionality of it; being able to feel the texture and weight of the amigurumi was such a thrill, after years of flat, two-dimensional digital work. Taking photographs of the amigurumi outside reminded me of what I liked most about making videos when I was younger—getting out and interacting with the world to tell stories. Crochet brought me back into the 3D world. As a kid, I remember wandering through the craft-store aisles and touching all the yarn. I'd ask my mom if she

Top: Howie Woo and Old Man Woo, from *Woo on Wheels* film, 2013, Old Man Woo: 9 x 3 in (22.86 x 7.62 cm). Photo: Howie Woo

Bottom: Howie Woo, *Robots are Poor Tippers*, 2010, crochet, 7 x 3 in (17.78 x 7.62 cm). Photo: Howie Woo

could make me something. Many years later, I'd bug my girlfriends to make me something out of yarn, particularly stuffed animals. When MJ started learning to crochet, she was interested in making scarves. So I thought, I should quit bugging people to make stuff for me and learn for myself.

Q: Woomi and Old Man Woo are reoccurring characters in your work. Are they your alter-egos?

A: Woomi is my alter-ego, yes. He's very different from me—he plays sports, drinks, smokes, and carouses. He represents my more impulsive side, I suppose. I felt like I needed a crochet version of myself to tell some of my real-life stories. But ultimately, Woomi became his own character. And now, the guy has his own spirit. There's even some competition between us. It's all very bizarre, like that feeling that ventriloquists get when they look at their puppets. It's amazing what we can infuse into inanimate objects, including the things we create. Old Man Woo is how I imagine myself in the future.

Q: How do you approach a story, particularly a longer piece such on *Woo on Wheels*?

A: *Woo on Wheels* came about from my fear of being too old or infirm to create. I started with the image of Old Man Woo in a wheelchair. I had a separate story in which I was a 1930s race car driver, and I ended up meshing those two stories together. The crocheting usually starts only after I've fleshed out the story with many sketches and scribbles.

Q: What's the story of Carrot Jetpack?

A: It started from my childhood desire to own a jetpack, but it seemed too easy to just make one. An object of desire can be boring without a backstory. So I wrapped it in a tale of espionage; I was recruited to test out the jetpack for surveillance purposes, and at the end of the mission, I handed out carrots to strangers on the street. Ultimately, it was all a prank organized by Woomi as revenge because I'd dressed him up as a rabbit. It is in moments like that where I feel that Woomi is his own character, out to get me!

Q: This espionage, spy-related story is something we are used to seeing in action movies and macho comic books, but you use wool to create the key item.

A: I never intended to use the traditional qualities of yarn-craft to counter male stereotypes. I'm a boy making stuff that, in general, boys like. In this case, and unexpectedly, it just happens to incorporate lots of yarn. I always wanted a jetpack and ray-guns and liked to pretend to blow up dynamite and be an action hero—all the typical boy stuff! At the same time, I'm a pretty artsy dude. So those contrasting forces show up in my blog. When I started it, I was very self-conscious about being a guy who crochets. But in no time, it became a non-issue. When I heard someone say, "Oh, you're the only guy I know who crochets," I would feel defensive. But if you spend a lot of time worrying about what other people think of you, you ultimately rob yourself of fun experiences that can be rewarding for yourself and others.

Top: Howie Woo, *Jetpack with Blue Skies*, 2011, yarn, fiber filling, cardboard, 25 x 16 in (63.5 x 40.64 cm). Photo: MJ Kuhn

Bottom: Howie Woo, *Raygun Ranger*, 2009, crochet, 9 x 8 in (22.86 x 20.32). Photo: MJ Kuhn

Howie Woo, *How the Fire Started, Toasting Waffles*, 2010, crochet 2.5 x 5 (6.35 x 12.7 cm). Photo: Howie Woo. Inspired by a news article about a condo that caught fire in Florida.

Q: Do you have any advice for fledgling storytellers who are looking for material?

A: I'd start off with true stories from your own past. After that, the imagination and flights-of-fancy eventually kick in!

Q: Is there anything else you'd like me to ask about your work?

A: I've started to teach myself computer programming this year, and I owe it all to the experience of learning basic crochet stitches. Applying existing artsy skills toward my projects gave me the confidence to dive into learning to write apps and games. Maybe my future apps will include some yarn creations. It's amazing how learning a new skill can lead to even more new skills because of the confidence that one gets during that process. I would encourage everyone to keep learning new things! ✳

How do you approach a subject with humor? Begin by working with the following ideas in your sketchbook before transferring your work to cloth.

1. Be specific.

2. Tell the truth in an entertaining way by challenging clichés or trying to dramatize them.

3. Examine what annoys you. How can you make suggestions, tongue-in-cheek or otherwise, for making the world a place that suits your needs?

4. Unsolicited advice is a gold mine for humor. What unwanted suggestions do others give you? Are some of them impossible to achieve or universally relatable?

5. What filters can you remove? Sometimes we concentrate so hard on trying not to offend others that we become too serious. Everyone has a different sense of what "funny" is. Stay true to what you find comedic.

Howie Woo, *Dynamite Danger*, 2009, crochet, 9 x 4 in (22.86 x 10.16 cm). Photo: Howie Woo

STITCHED REJECTION:

An Interview with Gina Dawson

Brooklyn-based artist Gina Dawson creates stitched replicas of objects that affect her life, including rejection letters from prestigious art institutions and receipts from Blockbuster video rentals. Gina's smart, self-deprecating work explores her relationship with celebrity, the language of rejection, and the passage of time.

Gina Dawson, *Consider Other Ways*, 2009, cut paper, 4 x 6 in (10.16 x 15.24 cm). Photo: Gina Dawson

Q: Tell me about yourself.

A: I'm originally from a small town in east Texas, but I like to think I have successfully acclimated to the north east; I live in Brooklyn. For a living, I oversee the making of high-end clothing in the New York City garment district as the director of domestic production. I can't take credit for the actual hand work of constructing these pieces, but I am proud of the finished items. As an artist, I make small, time-consuming objects where I do all the labor myself, and in turn, I also make a lot of mistakes.

Q: What sparked the idea for your stitched rejection letters?

A: I stitch souvenirs of my life. Like most of the things that I stitch, I choose these because I feel compelled to hold on to the original object. However, once I have created the stitched copy, I can throw away the original—which is a relief. The rejection letters were included among piles of things that I had felt were necessary to keep. As with most of my work, the idea started out as funny, but by adding hours of actual work, it become a proof of the failure, it became sort of sad, though—I hope—still funny in a way.

Q: You've also created companion funeral wreaths that are embroidered with quotes taken from the rejection letters. In your artist statement, you've said that both the letter and the wreath become "objects of consolation." What are you hoping that viewers will take away from this pairing?

A: When I was stitching the rejection letters, I found the language of rejection fascinating. These kinds of letters

Gina Dawson, *It Requires A Majority Vote*, 2009, cut paper, 4 x 6 in (10.16 x 15.24 cm). Photo: Gina Dawson

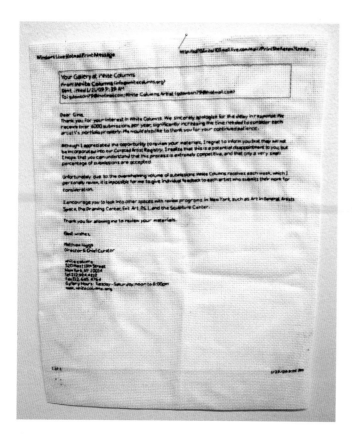

Gina Dawson, *Rejection Letter from White Columns*, 2009, fabric and thread, 8.5 x 11 in (27.94 x 21.59 cm). Photo: Gina Dawson

have a basic formula for placation, and naturally, they all fall short of actually achieving this. The concept that an anonymous letter will make you feel better about being a bad artist is as ridiculous as the idea that a tacky funeral wreath will make you feel better about death. Every time I get a rejection letter—to be melodramatic—I feel a little bit of the dream dies. The wreaths are little memorials to the tiny deaths by disappointments that artists endure.

Q: Your work has been described as having "self-deprecating humor." Do you agree?

A: I intend the work to be self-deprecating; I am advertising my shortcomings. I think that many artists can relate to this feeling. My rejection letters resonate with most, unless, of course, they have only known success.

Q: In 2008, you stitched *Movie Star Homes*, one of those star maps that visitors to Hollywood purchase in order to locate celebrity mansions. You've written that "knowing about and stitching stars makes them part of your life."

A: I stitched *Movie Star Homes* because I was interested in making something that, by the time I finished making it, would likely be out-of-date. Celebrities, like artists, fall in and out of favor. They also move house a lot. I'm sure that in the year that it took me to make the piece, some of the actors' addresses changed. Everyone on that map became very important to me, because I spent so much time with them. Celebrity and association to celebrities continue to fascinate me, as a lover of movies and television, and as someone who makes a living in the fashion world where celebrities have a huge influence on your brand's success.

When I made the piece in 2005, I was attending graduate school in Boston. I felt very much outside of the art world and the celebrity world. The stitching was done in isolation in my living room while I watched countless films and television shows about other people. The escapism of watching someone else's narrative was literally threaded to my present during that time. I felt as if they were, pardon the pun, intertwined. The map has evolved to represent something else to me now. Living in New York City, I feel more involved in the world of art and celebrity, but I also feel more jaded. I don't think I could "escape" into those other narratives now, and I don't think I'd actually want most of the people captured on the map to be part of my life. Although I'd probably still make an exception for Rod Stewart or LL Cool J!

Q: Why was it important to stitch Blockbuster video receipts in conjunction with making the star map?

A: If the map was fantasy, the receipts were the reality. I was sitting in my living room for eight to ten hours a day, often watching four to five movies at a time while I was working on the map. The receipts fell into the category of a testament to my existence, a daily souvenir. Stitching them after the map seemed the natural progression. They were also evidence of the time I spent making the one large object, which then spanned even more time. My art always seems to lead me to more "work." ✱

Gina Dawson, *Potential Disappointment*, 2009, funeral wreath made from cut paper, 4 x 6 in (10.16 x 15.24 cm). Photo: Gina Dawson

Project

#DadKnowsBest

IVIVA OLENICK

Iviva Olenick has designed a DIY project based on her embroidered poems project. She says, "This hand-embroidered piece is a poem written by my father for my @EmbroideryPoems project in which I compose, collect, and embroider tweet-length poems. My father has been a poet for many years. While he does not use Twitter, he enjoyed the linguistic challenge of composing one-liners for this project."

Picking Your Words

Iviva writes: "I've been embroidering excerpts of love stories and my own and others' confessions and secrets for years. I am increasingly interested in using social media as a collaborative art-making tool, and thought the challenge of composing 140-or-fewer-character poems would be fun and comical, hence @EmbroideryPoems was born. If you're not into poetry or Twitter, that's okay! This project is still for you. Maybe you have something you'd like to say to a loved one or a quote you rely on for self-encouragement. Embroidery can be a fun way to make tangible and permanent a fleeting thought or idea. That's what this project is about. It's also about finding humor in unexpected yet sometimes obvious places."

Start by identifying a funny quote, saying, or other snippet of text to translate into embroidery. This can be an excerpt of a text message or email exchange, a snippet of conversation, a line from a favorite poem, or a family saying.

CAUTION: Consider whether your embroidery will be made public online and/or will ever be for sale. Permission to use another person's text may become necessary or desirable from an etiquette and/or legal standpoint, so be prepared for that possibility. As an example, in @EmbroideryPoems, a separate agreement was made with each poet regarding the use of his/her poetry and the eventual potential sale and exhibit of the embroideries.

TOOLS & MATERIALS

- Text to embroider—the funnier, the better!—a tweet, a portion of a funny text message, a quote or a line of poetry; anything that inspires a laugh or a sense of hope or encouragement.

- 2.5 x 4-in (6.35 x 10.16-cm) light-colored woven fabric (cotton muslin or linen without too much texture)

- size 4 or 5 embroidery needle

- embroidery or sewing thread in a color that will be visible on the selected fabric.

  Note: #DadKnowsBest uses a single strand of cotton embroidery thread. It is possible to ply apart the thread and use 1 or 2 strands at a time instead of the entire thick floss.

- sewing scissors

- 6–8 in (15–20 cm) embroidery hoop

- iron and ironing board

- paper towel or fabric scrap

OPTIONAL MATERIALS

- graphic software such as Photoshop or Illustrator can be used to play with your design before committing it to fabric. Or you can go old-school by printing text on paper and cutting and pasting individual words into a pleasing layout. A third option is to sketch multiple versions onto paper.

- clear quilting ruler

- water-soluble marker.

  Note: Clover makes a fine point, light-blue, water-soluble marker that works well.

SKILLS

hand sewing

embroidery (backstitch, French knots)

WHEN WILL CHILDREN REALIZE
THEY'RE MORE OR LESS
JUST LIKE THEIR PARENTS
#DADKNOWSBEST

 Consider the look of the embroidered text—will it be cursive or print? Your own handwriting or a computer-generated font? Play with these options and the layout of the text either on the computer or by writing it out by hand on paper. For inspiration and ideas, see *dafont.com* for free, downloadable fonts. #DadKnowsBest is done in capital letters to reflect Dad's actual handwriting.

 Based on your experiments, determine placement of text. With a quilting ruler and water-soluble marker, draw several straight lines as guides for the text. Alternately, allow the text to meander in a less linear manner. You may even wish to skip writing out the text altogether, and improvise while embroidering.

TIP: If using a water-soluble marker, test it first on a corner of the fabric. It should wash out without soap, simply by running the fabric under water. Also, make sure thread color will not bleed if the fabric is washed or dampened by rubbing a sample of all threads between two fingers under running water.

Place the fabric in an embroidery hoop so that the start of the text is visible.

Thread a needle with 9–12-in (22–30-cm) length of thread. Knot end of thread and insert needle into fabric from underside along the first letter of text.

Use an embroidered backstitch to delineate the text, covering the handwritten letters in embroidery stitches. If the text is not handwritten beforehand, use the backstitch to start improvising the embroidery. The stitches on the back of the fabric may look disorganized. This is part of the process of using embroidery to render text. If desired, use French knots to render periods, colons, and/or semicolons, and to dot i's. If you use backstitch, just make smaller stitches for punctuation.

TIP: Round letters are easier to stitch if made with small stitches gently angled along the shape of the letter. If a letter just doesn't look as desired, it's okay to undo the most recent stitches and redo them, making adjustments for the size and placement of the stitches.

When text has been embroidered, remove embroidery hoop from fabric. Determine how much space/how large a border to leave around the text. Cut fabric accordingly, leaving at least 1 in (2.5 cm) extra fabric to fold under and stitch down, as if making a hem. (You may wish to leave an extra 0.25 in [6 mm] when trimming the fabric. If left un-hemmed, there will be ample room to fold under and stitch down the edges later, if desired.) Rinse fabric to remove evidence of the water-soluble marker.

Heat iron to an appropriate setting for the fabric. Use the iron to remove wrinkles and to sharpen folds around the edges. If fabric is damp, iron can help speed the drying process. Place a paper towel or piece of cloth over the back of the embroidery and gently iron back of piece.

Once fabric is dry and wrinkle-free, use backstitch to make a border around the fabric, framing the text and neatening up the edges of the fabric. Alternately, leave edges un-hemmed and let them fray; depending on the tone of the text, this may be an appropriate visual metaphor. Some types of fabrics tend to fray more than others.

☛ Hang your new stitched poem someplace where it can be admired!

Born and raised in Brooklyn, designer Iviva Olenick has exhibited her artwork in galleries and museums across the United States. Her art has been positively reviewed in *The New York Times*, *FiberArts*, and *Nylon* magazine. She holds a BA in Psychology and French Language and Literature from SUNY Binghamton, and an AAS in Textile and Surface Design from the Fashion Institute of Technology. Olenick has been awarded grants from the Brooklyn Arts Council and a BRIC Media Arts Fellowship, and is currently represented by Muriel Guepin Gallery in New York. *ivivaolenick.com*

Chapter Nine

TECHNOLOGY AND NEW METHODS OF STORYTELLING

We have a cult of efficiency. I think the DIY movement is a response to the digital age. I like my Mac, my phone, my digital camera, but embroidering gives me time to think.

—artist Bettina Matzkuhn

Social sharing

> *I really enjoy the way that the Internet has enabled an interest in knitting to spread much further. I love the way that so many knitters embrace technology.*
>
> —*artist Freddie Robins*

The digital world has brought about a variety of ways to communicate, including blogging, tweeting, and texting. Textile artists are exploring new technologies, weaving stories into QR codes that can only be read by a smartphone, re-creating Internet memes in their stitchwork, or journaling on fabric about online matchmaking. The urge to share our experiences through the handmade arts is not a notion lost in historical reference but a vibrant part of the community. Why shouldn't our textile work reflect how we communicate today?

Crafters have long embraced the opportunity to share stories about themselves and meet each other online. The popular website *Knithacker* asks knitters to submit images of items made from hacking two patterns together in order to create something "gloriously unique and knitty-licious." A community of *Knithacker* readers votes on what they think are the most successful knit hacks. Pattern sharing sites like *Ravelry.com* allow crafters to swap and disseminate their designs in a way that transcends international borders; the site has become a virtual test kitchen for knitting and crochet,

where one can see how a pattern has been made in hundreds of different yarn specifications, alterations, and gauges by other knitters. The way we learn to knit, weave, embroider, or crochet is changing too—new techniques can be picked up through online tutorials on YouTube or educational sites like *Skillshare*.

The ability to share images of work online proliferated with the craft blogging and yarn bombing movement, and crafters can now see what is being made halfway around the world. They can inspire each other through image-sharing sites like *Flickr*, *Instagram*, and *Pinterest*. Pink-collar e-commerce has emerged on crafting mega-retailer *Etsy* and proliferates in smaller sites such as *Big Cartel* and *Shopify*.

Maker workshops and hackspaces have also popped up, allowing for collaborations between those who make things by hand and those who are into technologies such as 3-D printers, electrical wiring, and computer code. The line between people who craft and those who do not is disappearing. It is not uncommon to see fields such as computing and textiles merging, to find fabric that contains conductive thread or a

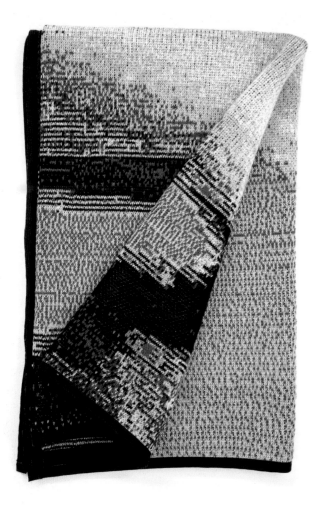

Phillip Stearns, *DCP_0242 Open Edition*, made in the US by Pure Country Weavers, 2013, 100-percent cotton, 53 x 71 in (134.62 x 180.34 cm). Photo: Phillip Stearns. Custom design made using a modified digital point-and-shoot camera.

character from a video game portrayed in some complicated intarsia knitting. Since 2011, the San Francisco Bay Area MakerFaire has hosted an e-textile lounge that highlights wearable technologies. Many of the garments shown in this space react to the environment, changing under variations of temperature, sound, or motion.

Technology gives us the opportunity to play with textiles in previously unexplored ways, and great opportunities exist to explore the relationship between how we share our human experience and how it is reflected back at us in the items that we choose to make.

Phillip Stearns' Beautiful Faults

In late 2011, Brooklyn-based artist Phillip Stearns started Glitch Textiles, a project dedicated to exploring the intersection between textiles and digital art. The patterns and designs of his machine-knit and woven wall hangings and blankets are based on glitches—technical processes that manifest as errors from digital cameras and other misused hardware and software. By capturing the hidden structures of data or the hallucinations of machines misinterpreting signals and weaving the resultant images, the digital experience is transformed into a sensory one. Stearns has transformed the "hard" world of binary, computational logic into soft and cozy textiles.

Canadian textile artist and educator Ruth Scheuing has been tracking her movements via GPS since 2005 and using these tracks as patterns that she incorporates into her weaving. (See *ruthscheuing.com*.)

Phillip Stearns, *DCP_0209 Knit Open Edition,* made in the US by Pure
Country Weavers, 2013, 100-percent cotton, 53 x 71 in (134.62 x 180.34
cm). Photo: Phillip Stearns. Custom design made using a modified digital
point-and-shoot camera.

Iviva Olenick, @EmbroideryPoems at their 61 Local Embroidery Slam debut, 2013, embroideries of various sizes on 24 x 18 in (60 x 45 cm) bulletin board. Photo: Michaele Olenick, a.k.a. Mom.

Poem credits: Top row from left to right: Angela Meyer (@candylecoque), Iviva Olenick (@EmbroideryPoems), Iviva Olenick, Lisa Kim (@lisakimlisakim). 2nd row: Iviva Olenick, Iviva Olenick, Melissa Broder (@melissabroder), Melissa Broder. 3rd row: Marcia Annenberg, Sandy Denarksi, Spencer Madsen (@spencermadsen). 4th row: Anonymous, Melissa Broder, Danielle Maveal (@daniellexo), Iviva Olenick. 5th row: Kevin Kinsella, Iviva Olenick. Final row: Montana Ray, Monte Olenick a.k.a. Dad, Monte Olenick, Elizabeth Rose Daly.

Iviva Olenick's @EmbroideryPoems

"For years, I've struggled with reconciling my desire to make things by hand with the threat of being 'left behind' in an economy and social scene driven by technology," explains Iviva Olenick. "As a result of these concerns, I've sought ways to use Facebook, Twitter, and Instagram in my art making." She's diarized her dating life on embroidered hankies, stitched her neighborhood jogging routes onto plastic shopping bags, and captured the letterforms of Brooklyn graffiti in French knots. In 2013, she started embroidering the tiniest of stories—140-character statements and poetry written via Twitter.

The technology of Twitter appealed to Iviva for several reasons. She said, "Twitter allows me to interact with people from all over the world and to collaborate without actually meeting face-to-face. The conciseness of the medium is appealing too. For years, I've been stitching epithets on scraps of discarded and recycled fabrics. The texts were often stream-of-consciousness, similar to the process of writing poetry. I felt as though I were saving scraps of my experience through stitch; hence, I used fabric scraps. Through Twitter, anyone can compose and broadcast to the world scraps of experience."

By combining other people's tweets with her embroidery, Iviva creates a link between Internet-based behaviors and craft as a communication tool. She has written, "I'm hoping to collapse the divide between technologically based socializing and marketing and the process of making objects by hand. Of course, there are still some very obvious differences, like the amount of time it takes to compose a tweet versus the time required to stitch one. I'm hoping that the process of making physical objects from tweets will encourage more thoughtfulness in terms of what we tweet."

Iviva has created thirty-three embroideries in the @EmbroideryPoems series, of which she says: "The physical act of writing down poetry is a way of making the intangible 'real.' Like poetry, tweets exist in a liminal, intangible space. I feel as though there is something poetic about tweets, even if they are not written as poems. Through embroidery, I capture these ethereal thoughts and moments, giving them a place to live."

In June 2013, she organized a poetry slam at the Brooklyn bar 61 Local. She invited her favorite poets and musicians and started the evening with an embroidery lesson. As the musicians performed, the embroiderers captured selected phrases with stitching, creating found poems.

To see more embroidered tweets, visit @EmbroideryPoems, *tumblr.com* or see pp. 205–06 to learn how to stitch your own embroidered poem.

THE SOCIAL KNITWORK

Lea Redmond's participatory project The Social Knitwork encourages knitters to create scarves that reflect the online interactions that they have with others. Using balls of wool in colors that represent popular sites Gmail, Pinterest, Blogger, Twitter, and Facebook, she knits a stripe to represent each status update created by her friends. The finished scarf becomes a record of social interactions online. As a community-engaged project, Lea encourages other knitters to try this pattern and offers a free download from her website as well as tips on how to use each social network. *leafcutterdesigns.com/projects/the-social-knitwork.html*

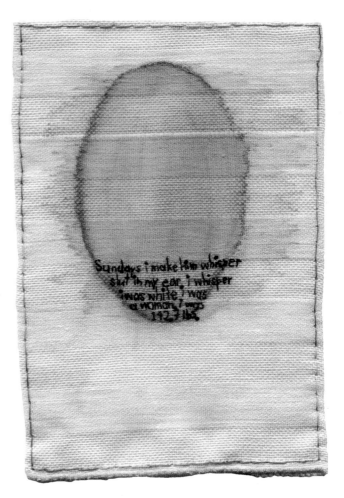

Iviva Olenick, *Sundays i make him whisper*, 2013, embroidery and watercolor paint on fabric with excerpt of poem by Montana Ray, 7.25 x 4.25 in (18.125 x 10.625 cm). Photo: Iviva Olenick

MIXING MEDIA:
An Interview with Kirsty Whitlock

Kirsty Whitlock is a textile artist based in Hampshire, UK, who produces limited-edition and one-off textile artworks. Her tactile, graphic, and powerful embroidery has become her signature along with upcycling discarded household items for her canvases. While using traditional techniques of stitching, her work brings into question our modern-day hunger for mixing imagery and message, akin to Internet memes and Creative Commons remixing. Kirsty uses her experimental embroidery to explore how textiles can be concerned with and comment on contemporary issues and affairs. In a world that is increasingly filled with altered and derivative works, Kirsty makes topical statements with her visual mash-ups of current affairs, embroidery, and the paper ephemera of modern consumer life. *kirstywhitlock.com*

Kirsty Whitlock, *Trash Talking*, 2009, ephemera, embroidery thread, dimensions unknown. Photo: Clare Catherine Kelly

Q: In your artist statement, you've said that your work "pushes the boundaries of embroidery through the use of materials and application," and that you'd like to "break preconceptions around textiles." Can you tell me more about this?

A: Embroidery is conventionally associated with women of an older generation and traditional cross-stitch patterns. Sadly, many people still view the sewing machine as a feminine domestic tool instead of as a powerful piece of machinery that has great potential to be used as a creative drawing and marking tool for all art and design disciplines. My work challenges such preconceptions through stitching on materials that were not normally associated with embroidery such as plastic carrier bags and newspapers. I explore contemporary issues and affairs and respond to them through experimental stitchwork while aiming to promote embroidery to a wider audience.

Q: What sparked the use of recycled and reclaimed material in your art? How do you source materials?

A: We are part of a disposable society. It seems cheaper to discard items and replace them with new ones than keep or repair them. I exploit the overlooked qualities of discarded household items with the aim of critiquing corporate culture and questioning our society's concept of value. My inspiration comes from newspaper headlines and documentaries. My use of materials ranges from milk-bottle tops to train tickets to plastic tape. I'm generally drawn to typography and color, and I'm always looking out for a new reusable material to work on. I source my materials in relation to the subject matter, and sometimes the found material can evoke the concept.

Q: I am curious about your works *Tomorrow the World* and *Bags of Aggro*, which I assume are related to each other.

A: *Bags of Aggro, Tomorrow the World,* and *Suffocation* all draw attention to the increasing visibility of giant supermarket chains both on the high street and in the media. The pieces aim to question what the rapid growth of the future holds for us—are supermarkets taking over the world? This tactile typography is inspired by newspaper headlines and mocks serious issues with playful humor and plays on words. For example, in the piece *Suffocation*, the printed text on the plastic carrier bag informs users of health and safety information. By using embroidery, I am highlighting the suffocation of communities by the giant supermarkets. The aim here is to critique corporate culture and raise issues and concerns about growth. These pieces have expressed a lot of opinions and emotions. Some viewers are able to relate to the issue closer to home with petitions and emotional locals fearing the loss of independent small businesses.

These pieces are made of layered plastic bags that have been deconstructed and reconstructed, and fused together. The typography extracted from newspaper headlines are stitched using machine embroidery with reference to the Great British flag featured within *Bags of Aggro*.

This collection of works was created in 2010 using biodegradable bags. In time, they will gradually begin to disintegrate. This process excites me, and I will be recording this change using photography. Will a skeleton of the stitch remain?

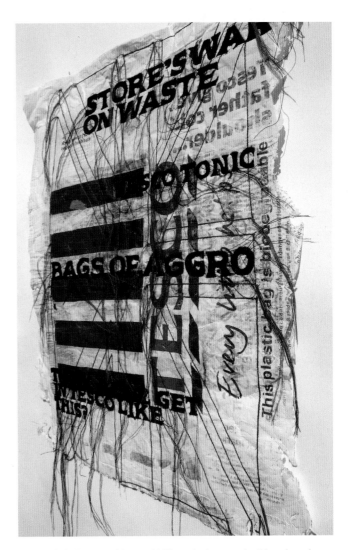

Kirsty Whitlock, *Bags of Aggro*, 2009 carrier bags, embroidery thread, dimensions unknown. Photo: Somayya Patel

Q: You have created some pieces related to the downfall of the world economy and financial sector, *Losses 2009* and *Meltdown Misery*. In *Losses 2009*, a copy of the *Financial Times* is deteriorating, held together with what looks like a mending stitch. Stock reports are embellished in satin stitches and red thread that literally cascades off the newspaper. In *Meltdown*, you've highlighted the rise and fall of the stock market with your stitching. What sort of reaction have you had to these pieces?

A: *Meltdown Misery* is a sample piece from a headline featured in the *Financial Times* that drew my attention. This experiment developed into *Losses 2009*, which was inspired by the economic climate at that time. With machine embroidery, I used the *Financial Times* to represent a significant period in time. This piece touches on how humor can get us through serious issues—if we weren't laughing about it, we would be crying. I want my work to be conversational and provoke the viewer's own opinions and emotions. Viewers often comment that "it looks how I feel—hanging on by a thread."

Q: You've written: "Embroidery has the power to transform; it enables the properties of materials to be manipulated, challenged, and subverted."

A: Embroidery has vast potential to be used as a creative drawing and mark-making tool. The process of embroidery allows you to investigate the surface qualities of the material and its context through techniques and conceptual ideas. It has the ability to transform, manipulate, and communicate a story.

In most of my pieces, I work with printed narratives and respond to the surface qualities of printed material as well as to the subject matter of the text. My work reflects both history and nostalgia. Embroidery creates a connection between the present and the past. My work tells a story of time. ✳

Kirsty Whitlock, *Losses 2009*, 2009, newspaper, embroidery thread, approximately 24 x 16 in (60.96 x 40.64 cm). Photo: Somayya Patel

Prompt

Think Outside the Sewing Box

1. Use digital media behavior for story-fodder: selfies, duck-face, drunken confessionals on Facebook, Klout score checking, Google Street View stalking, etc. While technology trends may come and go, how people are seen on the Internet is not that different from how they've been portrayed or projected in the past in high-school yearbooks or through graffiti in bathroom stalls. What timeless aspects of human behavior can be captured in your work?

2. Replicate online behavior in the real world. For example, can your work give someone or something an appreciative "like" in your work as you would on Facebook and Instagram? Can your work help to strengthen community?

3. Change your material and try something new—experiment with LED lights, pixels, strings of code, or reflective and heat-sensitive fibers.

4. Think about how your work can interact with the digital world. When the art collective Gelitin created a 200-ft (61-m) knitted rabbit, for example, it was seen on Google Earth.

FUZZY LOGIC:
An Interview with Carlyn Yandle

After seventeen years of working as a journalist, Carlyn Yandle decided to follow her dreams and enroll in art school. A lifelong crafter, she has brought a handmade sensibility to her conceptual practice. A graduate of Emily Carr University of Art and Design who identifies as an emerging artist, she has challenged the appropriation of symbols and copyright by VANOC (the Vancouver Organizing Committee for the 2010 Olympic and Paralympic Winter Games), created public commissions that brought textile motifs to heavy industrial construction, and explored technologies such as QR codes and Internet "networking" via textiles. Fearless in her approach, Carlyn utilizes crochet, sewing, knitting, and rug hooking in unexpected ways. Her defiant experimentation allows us to ponder how we communicate with each other through the confines of technology, corporatization, and social conventions.

Carlyn Yandle, *Wrap II*, 2013, poly building wrap, 100 in (254 cm) diameter. Photo: Carlyn Yandle

Q: How does your experience as a reporter influence the work that you've done as an artist?

A: I have this love-hate relationship with my background. What I learned in journalism was to really attract people to come into the conversation. I had a weekly column that was well read. I always started it with a personal anecdote as a hook, a way to entice people into the topic, which was usually a political issue. It is not the way that journalism is normally approached, and it was my trademark. Seventeen years of honing the ability to entice and engage, to tell and share—it's almost like a vice. In art, you want to keep things really open to the viewer.

Q: You've said, "I have to be able to speak about my work, but I have a pretty low tolerance for too much art-speak. I like artwork that has me at hello."

A: I went to see Nick Cave's *Soundsuits* at the Seattle Art Museum a couple of years ago. I was completely unprepared for what it was going to do to me. I walked in and I almost fell down. I just felt it—nobody was explaining it to me. If anybody had tried to explain it to me, I would have said, "Shut up, shut up! I'm having a moment!" I think I'm rebelling against any linear interpretation of an experience. I want to be able to just feel it in my stomach first.

Q: Can you tell me about *Logo Sweater*?

A: I was watching the news unfold in the months before the 2010 Vancouver Winter Olympics. There was a dispute between the Cowichan band and the Hudson's Bay Company. The Hudson's Bay Company wanted to make

Carlyn Yandle, *Logo Sweater*, 2010, un-worsted buffalo yarn, dimensions approximately 16 x 28 in (40.64 x 71.12 cm). Photo: Carlyn Yandle

THE COWICHAN BAND

is the largest First Nations band in British Columbia, Canada. The Cowichan sweater involves a style of knitting similar to Fair Isle. The sweaters are knit with patterns created by Cowichan women, with thick, neutral-colored, hand-spun wool. In Canada, they are considered special objects that can be created only by women of the Cowichan tribe.

knitted sweaters using the Cowichan band's patterns, but get them mass-produced in China. The Cowichan band claimed ownership of the sweaters and said this was appropriation. I started to think about what would happen if you appropriated the Hudson's Bay Company logo. What if you appropriated all the logos of the Olympics? What's allowed and not allowed? If you put it into a garter stitch or a stocking stitch, how far can you push trademark violation or appropriation without getting into trouble?

Q: What were the sort of reactions the *Logo Sweater* got in public?

A: Douglas Coupland wore it. My brother wore it a few times. The choirmaster for a political-song choir called Solidarity Labour Notes wore it. What was really interesting was that wearing a handmade sweater became a tiny act of rebellion. I didn't want to be really obvious about my political intentions for that sweater. I wanted it to walk a fine line in terms of getting everybody annoyed. I imagine the Cowichan band would have been mad because I used Cowichan-style wool and designs.

Q: What inspired *QR Quilt*?

A: I was interested in the idea of translations. This is a translation of a Douglas Coupland work that is a blend of QR codes and abstract expressionist painting. When you scan it, it goes to the title of his painting, which is called *I wait and I wait and I wait for God to appear.*

Q: Tell me about *Seismic Rug.*

A: I have made a million braided rugs before. I love the idea that you can use fabric even after it's too deteriorated to use for quilting. You take all that almost-gone fiber, tighten it all up through braids, and sew it up again.

I watched the aftermath of the 2011 tsunami in Japan on television. I'd lived in Japan for almost two years, so it was heady stuff to me. I had sciatica at the time, and I was down on my stomach in sphinx pose for two weeks, and I couldn't really do anything, so I started braiding a rug to deal with my tension and avoid watching this horrible footage, but I was compelled to watch it at the same time. As I was working, I started to think about the epicenter of the tsunami, which is like a giant stone dropped into water with big huge concentric rings. I wanted to build that shape into this ring-form rug.

Q: You've also designed public works inspired by textiles, like the *Crosswalk Scramble,* or the manhole cover with the doily design on it.

A: I like to use textiles in the material or the concept to mess with any jurisdictions or boundaries between the interior, domestic, low crafts and high art or industry. I just loved watching these big burly guys embedding my fiber design in the tarmac. These big men were basically making a big doily.

....

Top right: Carlyn Yandle, *QR Code Quilt: After Douglas Coupland,* 2013, found business shirts, cotton fabrics, buttons, approximately 72 x 90 in (182.88 x 288.6 cm). Photo: Carlyn Yandle

Bottom right: Carlyn Yandle, *Seismic Rug,* 2011, rag rug, found fabrics, 60 x 6 in (152.4 x 15.24 cm). Photo: Carlyn Yandle

Carlyn Yandle, *Crossover*, 2012. Photo: Carlyn Yandle. A scramble crosswalk design motif based on the weave of fishermen's nets in Steveston, British Columbia.

I was the editor of the newspaper in Steveston, British Columbia, for four years where the crosswalk scramble is installed, so I had a pretty good understanding of the history in that area, where there's a Japanese fishing and net-making industry. There were huge net lofts there, and all of it was handwork. The idea of a crosswalk was also a safety net for people.

Q: You also have an interactive fiber sculpture project called *The Social Network* that you created "with people who like to connect in the actual world."

A: I started this project in conjunction with Debbie Westergaard Tuepah, who was my studio-mate at the time. People stay at home alone, but they're on Facebook "networking." We thought there was a logic gap here. People who make things love to get together for stitch 'n' bitches or knitting circles, sewing circles, or quilting bees. What if we created a project in which people interact with each other and with fiber, and they didn't have to know any special skills? It's easier to let the conversation flow if your hands are at work. We originally thought of it as a macramé project, but people just did what they wanted to. We accepted that as human nature and shifted our roles from trainers in basic knotting technique to IT-type trouble-shooters who could ensure a good connection for however people attached the synthetic fabric strips. The parallels between this project and social media thicken as this thing progresses. As it grows, the snarled densities remind us of the storm of viral topics, and dangling threads seem like visuals to dropped conversations that have the potential to be picked up again. The bright colors start to reference fiber-optic cables, and the limitlessness of the project reflects infinite human interaction.

We tracked the progress in an ongoing blog, where we also added names of people who "tie one on" or literally join a thread in the conversation, if they give us their permission. People kept asking, "What's the right way? What's the correct way?" And we were like, "There is no correct way." If there were broken connections, later we'd go in and fix them like IT people would, but we tried not to ruin the integrity of how the thing was going. It's just a really fun social-engagement project. We have a dream that it will be installed in a gallery and people come and keep working on it. It could be a life-long project.

Q: Is there any work that I haven't asked you about that you want to tell me?

A: I did one series called Fuzzy Logic working with fractal forms...I've used that technique on a huge tarp that my brother dragged out of the rainforest. I loved the color variations, all these different blues, and the fact that it was almost not held together at all. It was almost disintegrating...I created this hyperbolic crochet with a giant needle, and I made a huge spore. I like this connection between the tarps that you see all over Vancouver for leaky condos and all that black moldy spore stuff that we're trying to keep away even though we're basically living in a rainforest.

The piece *Spore* was in the World of Threads international textile symposium show in Toronto in 2012. It was a big breakthrough for me to be able to get a weird thing in and for people to say, "This is not weird, this is awesome!" That was a real turning point for my art. ✳

Top: Carlyn Yandle, *The Social Network* at Vancouver Mini Maker Faire, 2012. Photo: Carlyn Yandle

Bottom: Carlyn Yandle, *Spore* from the Fuzzy Logic series, 2011, tarp, 18 x 30 x 10 in (45.72 x 76.2 x 25.4 cm). Photo: Carlyn Yandle

Project

Hello, World! Blinky Light Lilypad Arduino Patch

EMILY SMITH

Hello, World! is a felted and blinking LED brooch that reflects the skills that designer Emily Smith picked up from the crafting and hacker communities that she's involved in, both online and in person. She learned how to needle-felt from an exhibitor at Maker Faire in San Francisco and acquired a basic understanding of how to use an Arduino, an open-source electronic prototyping platform that comes with reactive hardware, from members of the hackerspace that she belong to in Vancouver, British Columbia.

"I learned about conductive thread from online forums," Emily says. "I had been researching its properties and then I started to make things with it. This project is a great beginner exercise to learn how to program the Arduino. Once you've made some lights blink in Hello, World!, the possibilities of what you can accomplish are very far-reaching. After visiting our local hackerspace in Vancouver, I opened my mind up to the idea of modifying the technology we consume. In the programming world, the phrase 'Hello, World!' is used to illustrate to beginners the most basic syntax of a programming language."

TOOLS & MATERIALS

- There are a number of Arduino Lilypads in production. Any one of the following Lilypad types will work for this project (which uses the Lilypad Simple):

    i) Lilypad Arduino USB* (recommended model)
    arduino.cc/en/Main/ArduinoBoardLilyPadUSB

    ii) Lilypad Simple* (the model used in the example)
    arduino.cc/en/Main/ArduinoBoardLilyPadSimple

    Note: Lilypad Simple requires the purchase of a separate USB add-on available from *sparkfun.com/products/10275*

*Both the Lilypad Arduino USB and Simple can be powered by a lithium ion polymer battery. A charger is required for the lithium ion polymer battery. *nicegear.co.nz/batteries-chargers/lithium-ion-battery-110mah/*

iii) Lilypad Arduino: *arduino.cc/en/Main/ArduinoBoardLilyPad*

Note: The Lilypad Arduino requires a separate power supply. The addition of an extra board can be a bit cumbersome, which is why the Lilypad Arduino USB is recommended. The power supply can be purchased through Sparkfun (*sparkfun.com/products/11259*).

- Lilypad LEDs (white) (available from *sparkfun.com/search/results?term=lilypad+LED&what=products*)

- 1 USB cable

- 2.18 yd (2 m) conductive thread (available from *sparkfun.com/products/10867*).

  Note: conductive thread generates an electrical current through fabric.

- sewing needle

- needle-felting needle

- computer installed with Arduino software (free to download at *arduino.cc/en/Main/Software#toc1*). The Arduino software is compatible with computers running Windows, Mac OS X, and Linux.

- code to program your Arduino Lilypad.

  Note: The code used in Hello, World! can be downloaded from *leanneprain.com/strangematerial/downloads* and uploaded to your Lilypad. You will need to cut and paste this, or other code, into the Arduino software on your computer in order to make the LED lights blink in succession.

- foam pad

- 200 g (7.05 oz) felt roving

- 1 sheet felt, used to back the brooch

- safety pin

- 10-in (25.4-cm) length Velcro

- sewing scissors

SKILLS

- sewing

- needle felting

- basic understanding of electronics and electronic components

- trouble-shooting skills

- basic understanding of how to program using Arduino software

- basic understanding of electronics

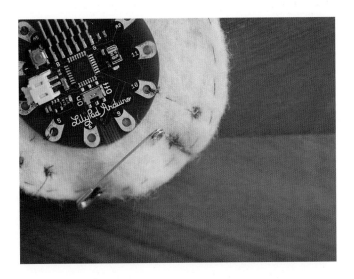

MAKE YOUR LILYPAD

1. Sketch design on paper or make it up on the fly. Consider basic circuit construction when creating your image.

   Note: If you wish to felt fiber over the LEDs as part of your design, note first where the + and − connections are as per the Circuit Diagram.

2. With sewing scissors, cut 2 shapes from the felt that will form the background of the brooch and the backing of Lilypad. Arrange felt roving on this felt base as you'd like it to appear.

3. Sculpt an image onto patch by stabbing the felting needle into the felt roving with felting needle. (The burrs on the needle tangle fibers together, which make felt denser so that you can fuse sections together or shape your image.) Try techniques like rolling felt roving to create desired shapes. (See p. 229.) Emily made a felted snail for her brooch, but you can choose any image that appeals to you.

4. Using the conductive thread, sew the LED lights onto the image, taking the circuit diagram into consideration. Make sure to look closely at the plus (+) and minus (−) notation on each LED marked by each hole (where you will sew LED onto fabric). Sew the + and the − to corresponding sections on the board

5. Trim conductive thread close to knots to ensure that there is no interference between electric currents.

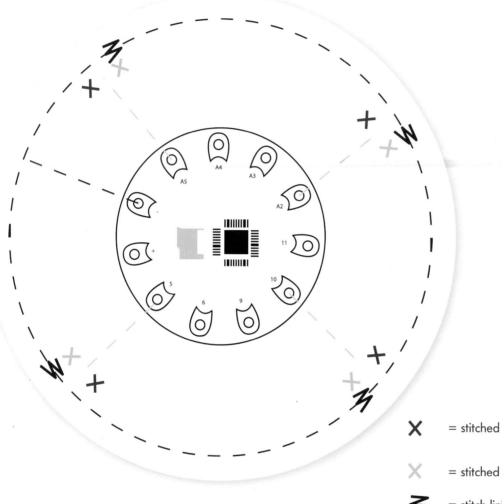

X = stitched LED (+)

X = stitched LED (−)

Ʒ = stitch linking LED to ground

- - - = link to ground on arduino board (−)

- - - = link to (+) markers on board

Photos: Emily Smith

6. Both sides of the LEDs require multiple layers of conductive thread in order to confirm the connection. Stitch over them several times. This stitching is the first step to connect LEDs to Lilypad.

7. Attach Lilypad to back of brooch. Notice holes around edge of device where you will sew conductive thread. While the numbers on different Lilypad models vary, all Lilypads have a "ground" lobe, labeled on the left of the diagram, and indicated by a – sign. Every other node on the Lilypad conducts a positive + charge. The "ground" is a safety implementation used in most electronics that creates a path for unintended electrical current to travel, thereby keeping you and your electronics safe from static or other types of electricity. To complete a circuit, it needs a positive (+) terminal and negative (–) terminal, and the circuits need to be connected in the right order.

8. In the circuit diagram (*circuitdiagram.ai*), note that the – mark on each LED draws a line to this "ground" or – charge on the Lilypad. To conduct electricity to the –, link all of the – charges on LEDs to this ground by sewing a line of conductive thread that connects all LEDs.

9. Ensure that you link all positive charges to the closest + lobes on the Lilypad as you sew with conductive thread.

10. Connect project to a USB cable and plug into your computer. If you are using the Lilypad Simple model, you will need an external adapter. Make sure to turn the switch on the Lilypad to the on position. You will first use the Arduino software to test that all of your LED lights work. Open the downloaded program from the Arduino website, then cut and paste the "blink code" from this webpage *arduino.cc/en/Tutorial/Blink#.UwF93kJdV7E*. From the Arduino software, click the arrow (it looks like a "play" button) to upload the code. If the Lilypad is working correctly and the LEDs are attached correctly, it will blink a light on the board when you've plugged it into your computer's USB port—success! If you notice a red light on your Lilypad, this means that your Lilypad is talking to the Arduino software and may need a few moments to load.

11. Keeping the Arduino Lilypad plugged into the computer, upload Hello, World! code from *leanneprain.com* by opening the downloaded file with Arduino software. To open the code, click the arrow on the left of the screen to upload code to the device.

    Note: This stage of the process may involve some online troubleshooting, and this may be a good time to ask for help at your local hacker (or maker) space (see *hackerspaces.org/wiki/List_of_Hacker_Spaces*). If you are having trouble getting a light to blink, it may be because your stitches need a stronger contact between your stitch lines and the link to the Lilypad or the LED.

12. Protect the circuit board by adding a piece of Velcro to the back of patch. Attach a safety pin to the top of the Velcro. Cut a slice for the safety pin to pass through.

13. Once you have unplugged Arduino from the computer, you will need a standalone battery to power it and keep the LEDs going. See the Tools & Materials list on p. 224–25 to see what sort of battery your type of Arduino will need. Follow manufacturer's instructions for installing the battery.

Turn your Lilypad on to see the lights blink (use the tiny on/off switch on the circuit board). Don't forget to turn it off when you are done to conserve power! Your Lilypad brooch will retain this program indefinitely, or at least until you plug it back into your computer and upload different code to the Arduino software.

Now that you have the basic tools to Arduino programming, there is no limit as to what can be accomplished with the Arduino!

Note: Hello, World! code written by Vincent van Haaff.

Emily Smith is an avid textile artist, community organizer, maker, teacher, and communication designer. She is co-founder of Vancouver Mini Maker Faire, founder of Vancouver Maker Foundation, and a contributor to MAKE Magazine. Her driving purpose is to connect and inspire a community of makers to invigorate industry, art, and education in Vancouver. In her spare time, she enjoys knitting, spinning, weaving, swimming, bicycling, and learning to play the banjo. *bluemollusc.com*

Chapter Ten

COMMUNITY STORYTELLING THROUGH TEXTILES

Our stories are reflections of ourselves. Treat them with respect and honor those who are willing to share their experiences with you.

—artist, community activator, and Yarn Bomb Yukon Collective coordinator Jessica Vellenga

Collective experience

Our good friends would go to the bus stop in Cleveland with a bunch of
S.T.I.T.C.H.E.D pieces and sit there, sewing by hand. People waiting at the
bus stop would ask what they were doing, and they'd reply, "Tell us a story!"

—*Alixa Garcia from Climbing PoeTree*

While much of this book has explored stories told by an individual artist or author, textiles have long been at the center of community life. When a textile, such as a quilt or a yarn bombing, is claimed by a community and used to tell a shared story, the end result is a conduit of many hands and minds. By contributing to a larger work that reflects a collective experience, an individual can express themselves while also entering a context of shared ownership. Community stories reflect a different sort of history than those collected by news sources or published in history books.

I do arts and crafts that are community-focused with young people because I think it's important for them to see intergenerational activity.

—*artist Marion Coleman*

NAMES Project AIDS Memorial Quilt

In June 1987, a group of San Franciscans, spearheaded by gay-rights advocate Cleve Jones, met to discuss a way to create a memorial to their friends, family members, and lovers who had died of AIDS. The initial meeting sparked the creation of what is now known as the NAMES Project AIDS Memorial Quilt. First shown in 1988 at the National Mall in Washington, DC, the quilt took up more square footage than a football field and consisted of more than 1,920 panels. Each panel in the quilt is handcrafted and measures six by three feet (1.83 x 0.91 m), the size of an average human casket.

Since its debut, the quilt has grown to be the largest community art project in the world. In 1989, it was nominated for a Nobel Peace Prize. It currently contains more than 48,000 panels, each commemorating someone who has died of AIDS-related illness. If a viewer spent one minute to view each panel on the quilt, it would take thirty-three consecutive days to see every panel in the project.

Each panel is accompanied by letters, biographies, and photos chronicling the pandemic in a way that is, in the words of the organizers, "on very real, very human terms." This project has redefined collective quilt-making in contemporary times and serves to memorialize many of those who were discriminated against during their lives. New patches are being added as the NAMES project receives them.

The NAMES Project Foundation has begun an Archive Project. Each panel in the quilt is analyzed for visual and historical content and will be added to a digital database. Other materials are being collected for an oral database. The quilt itself has become a wonderful historical record of human life and offers researchers the opportunity to explore rural heritage, textile histories, African-American history, and twentieth-century milestones of American life.

Circles of Stitching

From quilting bees to sewing circles, talking while you make something by hand is a wonderful way to socialize. For centuries, the sewing circle was where women could convene and speak their minds in a private sphere, away from men. In fact, one of North America's oldest sewing circles, the Fragment Society in Boston, was incorporated in 1816 (after forming in 1812) so that it could hold and dispose of property. Incorporation provided a loophole in the property laws for married women who could not own property apart from their husbands. Through incorporation, a sewing circle could hold property. Founded to "assist in clothing the destitute," the Fragment Society still functions as a charitable women's organization that celebrated 200 years in October 2012. Sewing circles were also popular in Mennonite communities, and were recorded in Eastern Pennsylvania as early as 1895, spreading quickly from one Mennonite community to another.

Knitting circles, colloquially known as stitch 'n' bitches, became popular during the 1940s with women who gathered to stitch and chat about their daily lives. In the early 2000s, these groups experienced a resurgence in popularity among young women after the release of Debbie Stoller's Stitch 'n Bitch books. Knitters (and crocheters) began to gather in circles again to bitch and to stitch, and held their meetings not only in homes and yarn shops, but in bars, pubs, roller derby rinks, and subway cars.

In 2001, in Calgary, Alberta, Grant Neufeld found a Revolutionary Knitting Circle that was quickly copied by others throughout Canada, the US, and parts of Europe. One of the group's first well-known projects was the Global Knit-in during the 2002 G8 Summit in Alberta. To protest corporate power, the Revolutionary Knitting Circle called on knitters to create "soft barriers of knitted yarn to reclaim spaces from the elite for the common good." By actively seeking members of various genders, ages, and classes, they refuted the concept of the stitching circle as a domestic, feminized craft and reclaimed it as a symbol of community, homespun values, and independence.

Other versions of stitching circles include crafternoons, in which people come together to make things, and hackspaces where technologists and crafters learn from each other. Each carry on the time-honored tradition in which people gather to make in one another's presence.

Putting a Community in Stitches

Since the 2012 Summer Olympics in London, there have been a number of wildly popular yarn bombings in North Yorkshire, England. A group of mystery knitters in the seaside town of Saltburn have delighted local residents and the world with a series of complex yarn bombings. The first was a fifty-foot (15.24-m) piece of knitting wrapped around the Saltburn Pier. Three-dimensional knitted figurines, each representing an Olympic sport such as swimming, football (soccer), and cycling, were placed every few feet along the pier.

The group chose to keep their identity anonymous, save for the codename Darn Crazy. Local residents have chosen to respect their anonymity and have applauded the knitters for bringing attention to the town and tourists to local businesses. Two other pieces of artwork have cropped up on the Saltburn Pier since the piece of Olympic proportions. In May 2012, an installation of knitted crowns, corgis, and princesses celebrated Elizabeth II's Diamond Jubilee. One year later, Darn Crazy returned with a yarn bombing that celebrated the town itself with an installation of all things seaside: fishermen, seagulls, burnt sunbathers, kelp, seashells, ice cream cones, and even knitted fish and chips.

Darn Crazy, *Saltburn Installations*, 2012, knitting and crochet, dimensions unknown. Photo: Anonymous

Darn Crazy, *Saltburn Installations*, 2012, knitting and crochet, dimensions unknown. Photo: Anonymous

If you are a crafter or maker of any kind, I highly recommend that you look up your local hackerspace at hackerspace.org. Check it out and participate in events, or create some of your own.

—crafter and Vancouver Hackerspace member **Emily Smith**

START A STITCHING CIRCLE

To start your own stitch 'n' bitch, you need just four things:

1. People: You can start a stitching circle with as little as two people, but more people means more fun. Use social media, the web, and community bulletin boards to get the word out.

2. Place: A coffee shop, a local pub, a meeting room in the library, a classroom, or your living room are all great places to gather, though places that provide food and drink will always win Brownie points. If meeting at a local business, clear the time in advance with the owner and pick an off-peak hour.

3. Craft: Some groups are for purists (knitting-only), and some allow needle-felters, crocheters, and tabletop weavers to mingle. Decide what works best for your group dynamics.

4. Time: Decide how often you will meet—once a week or once every few months—just be consistent. Two hours is usually the right length of time for each meeting.

Community Building, One Bridge at a Time

In Pittsburgh, Pennsylvania, more than 1,900 volunteers came together to cover the massive Andy Warhol Bridge with a yarn bomb that lasted from August 12 to September 6, 2013. Spearheaded by Amanda Gross with assistance from crocheters and knitters and the Fiber Arts Guild of Pittsburgh, this community created 600 blankets to cover the 1,001-foot (305.10-m)-long bridge. When the installation was removed, the handcrafted pieces found a second life as blankets donated to emergency shelters, nursing homes, and animal advocacy groups. *knitthebridge.wordpress.com*.

Amanda Browder's Future Phenomena

Brooklyn-based artist Amanda Browder facilitated a community sewing and installation project called *Future Phenomena*. In this single-day event, a fabric structure covered the entire façade of a local apartment building. The fabric was donated by residents of the neighborhood and by Wearable Collections, a community recycling group in New York. The piece was constructed by local sewing groups who gathered together in church basements to sew the colorful panels together. The final public installation celebrated the spirit of volunteerism, and the end result was the effort of an entire community. *amandabrowder.com*

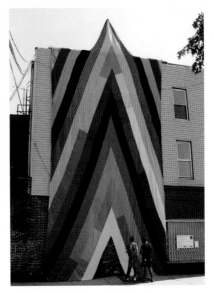

Top: *Knit the Bridge*, yarn bombing of Andy Warhol Bridge, Pittsburgh, 2013. Photo: Annette Sandberg

Bottom: Amanda Browder, *Future Phenomena*, 2010, recycled and reclaimed fabrics. Photo: Amanda Browder

HARNESSING THE POWER OF THE STITCH COMMUNITY:

An Interview with Leigh Bowser

Leigh Bowser is a twenty-four-year-old crafter, aunt, and artist living in Leeds, West Yorkshire, England. Her Blood Bag Project invites people to stitch a textile version of a blood bag. Leigh holds a BA in Textile Crafts from the University of Huddersfield in the UK, with a concentration in embroidery. She sells free-motion, machine-embroidered brooches on Etsy under the moniker LeighLaLovesYou. *thebloodbagproject.com*

The Blood Bag Project, *Portrait of Chloe*, 2012. Photo: Leigh Bowser

Q: When your niece Chloe was diganosed with a rare blood condition (Diamond Blackfan Anemia or DBA) that required many transfusions, you were unable to donate blood yourself, but started a project that would inspire others to do so. What is your goal for the Blood Bag Project?

A: Crafting is a way of allowing those who cannot donate or who want to do more to have an opportunity to help. By spending time crafting something with their own hands, it gives them time to reflect on why they're making what they are making. Crafters are invited to make their own textile blood bag by visiting the project's website and downloading the free PDF template. Over 260 bags have been created so far. Participants are young and old, novice and experienced crafters from all over the world. The bags have been on exhibition a few times now, and I hope to get them exhibited again. If more people can see the bags, then more are likely to learn something and respond—hopefully by donating blood.

DBA is so rare that no one has heard of it. If one person learns about DBA through the project and tells one other person about what they're making, that's two people who now know about this rare condition. It's a snowball effect, and I'm so happy that, because of the project, at least 260 people now know what Diamond Blackfan Anemia is. If just one person has seen the project and became a regular blood donor, then I feel my goal has been reached. I want people to be inspired to do something that is as easy as blood donation, but which can literally change and save lives.

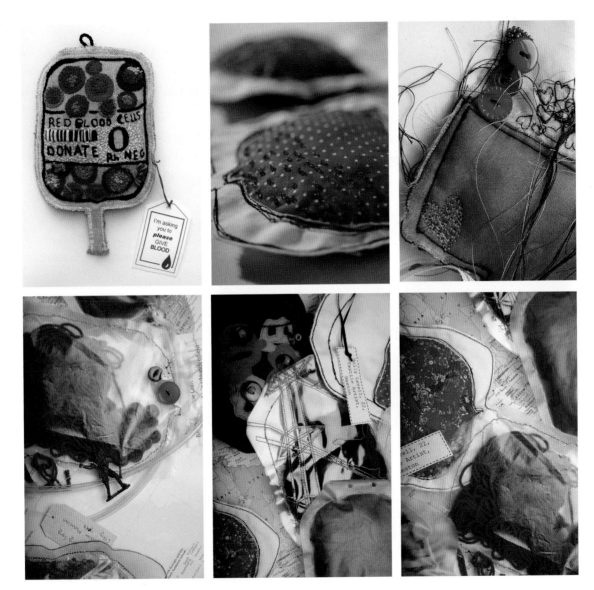

Various artists, the Blood Bag Project, 2012. Photos: Leigh Bowser

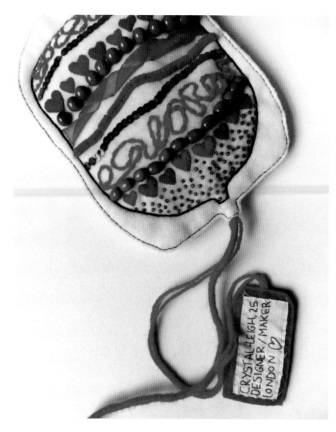

Crystal Leigh, the Blood Bag Project, 2012. Photo: Leigh Bowser

Q: You've received artwork from America, Australia, Switzerland, and Spain. Are there cultural differences in how people from different countries interact with this project?

A: The project is a universal story—absolutely anyone can relate to it. I'd bet nine-tenths of people know someone who has needed a blood transfusion. Although the process of blood donation differs from country to country, it's been nice to hear that contributors have given blood, as well as creating their textile bags. A few have had blood transfusions themselves and therefore can't donate, so it's lovely to hear they are using the project as a way to say thank you, to give back.

Q: Do you have any advice for someone who may want to stage a community project or a storytelling project?

A: Don't be afraid to just go for it. If you're passionate about it, it will be reflected in your work. Also, I recommend setting up a blog. You can instantly reach a worldwide audience at the click of a button, and you'll be surprised at how quickly people will respond—it's amazing! ✳

HOW TO DESIGN A COMMUNITY TEXTILE PROJECT

Discovery: Find the story that you want to tell. Will your project tell a single story embraced by a community or will it be a collection of stories? Find some like-minded allies and brainstorm ideas. Collaborating with others will bring out new ideas and solidify the purpose of your project.

Skill-sharing: Decide on whether this project will be made with skills that can easily be taught to anyone who wants to join in (finger-knitting and basic straight-stitch embroidery are effective but simple) or if it requires an advanced skill set (quilting and weaving, for example, have a steep learning curve).

Co-conspirators: Spread the word about your project through community newspapers, blogging, social media, postering in your community, and good old-fashioned word-of-mouth.

Design: Color, texture, fabric type, technique, shape—decide on a few common elements that will tie your project together.

Creation: Allow people to help you make items. Host crafting sessions at your local craft store, library, or coffee shop.

Installation: Where will the story be installed? Will it be a surprise that pops up overnight, or is it something that a community will come together and participate in building?

Documentation: How will this story be captured? Will it be photographed so that images can be shared long after the project is over? Will the participants be interviewed for an audio or visual archive?

Lifespan: Is it a limited-time project or one that could live in the community for a long time? Will it be lent to various members of the community for periods of time? Will it be dismantled and recycled into something else? Will members of the community be able to reclaim their contributions? Will pieces be sold off for charity?

COMMUNITY CONFESSIONS:
An Interview with Jessica Vellenga

Based in Whitehorse, Yukon, Jessica Vellenga is a textile artist who focuses on community engagement in both her practice and her work at the Yukon Arts Center Public Art Gallery. She creates collaborative, participatory projects for her community. Working in-between craft, art, and activism, her practice is grounded in the craftivism movement. She is the coordinator of Yarn Bomb Yukon, a collective that creates yarn bombing works (including one that covered a DC-3 plane) and hosts classes and presentations. *jessicavellenga.com*

Jessica Vellenga, *I Was Always Nauseated at the Sight of Bobby Pins*, 2012, embroidery on vintage textile, dimensions unknown. Photo: Douglas Drake

Q: Tell me about *Dear Diary*.

A: It's a community-based art project that celebrates the tradition of the diary. The project began during my residency at the Klondike Institute of Art and Culture in Dawson, Yukon, in October 2012. I asked the public to anonymously send me diary entries through my blog, social media, or by email. I then embroider these anonymous diary entries onto vintage and antique textiles. The project was inspired by reading my own old diary entries and other diaries and memoirs. It celebrates the banal, pivotal, silly, sad, and serious records that we keep. By disclosing the private to the public and sharing our stories, we create an experience of empathy for the viewer. I have received diary entries from across North America. It's a work in progress, and I will continue to solicit entries and expand the series.

Q: What was it in your diaries that inspired you? What made you want to turn to others to collect their stories?

A: From the progress of my own life from childhood into adulthood, my diary is a reminder of the moments chosen to be worthy of a written record. As we grow and change, so does the information that we choose to record. I wanted others to contribute [to the project] to show the commonalities that we all share in our daily lives.

A lot of my work, including this series, is based on shared experience and focuses on evoking empathy and giving strength by sharing our stories. I'm interested in personal stories and the concept that the personal is political, that individual stories reflect the global culture.

Q: Do you have any favorite entries?

A: "Take smart risks and never trust bears" was advice on northern living given to me when I lived in Dawson. While it applies to my personal fear of bears, I also like the concept of taking smart risks. One of the more historic entries, from the 1930s, states: "A woman to be happy…must be busy, and she must be good company when alone with herself. 'Content' is a matter of content." I think that one is still relevant. One of my favorites was from a woman who had kept a calendar journal every year from 1965 until the end of her life in 2010. I appreciated the simplicity and dedication to writing something every day—and within the confines of one square inch per day. Another favorite was from a woman who had posted her diary entries from grade six online, spelling mistakes and all. They were quite amusing but also a very honest account.

Q: Tell me a bit about your design process and the techniques you use to capture these stories.

A: I have a large collection of vintage and antique textiles. I like to use textiles that echo the sentiments or era of the diary entries. Sometimes I illustrate them as a way to enhance the statements. To stitch the text, I hand wrote all the entries with a water-soluble transfer pen. The embroidery, like handwriting, is unique and slightly imperfect. I keep all of the entries authentic and intact in their original format, without editing or censoring them. ✳

Top: Jessica Vellenga, *I Want the Real Me to Be Seen and for Somebody to Think It Is Good*, 2012, embroidery on vintage textile, dimensions unknown. Photo: Douglas Drake

Jessica Vellenga, *Take Smart Risks and Never Trust Bears*, 2012,
embroidery on vintage textile, dimensions unknown. Photo: Douglas
Drake

Spinning Stories:
Participatory Art with Robyn Love

Artist Robyn Love has exhibited at internationally renowned art galleries and museums, but some of her most intriguing work has occurred in places as mundane as a subway car. Her interest in creating site-specific work has led to her use of textiles to collaborate in ways that result in spontaneous acts of storytelling between herself and strangers. Robin said, "My performances are always participatory and thus lead to unexpected outcomes. Impossible to rehearse, they take advantage of what is possible when an idea is offered spontaneously to a group of people."

In April 2012, Robyn created a performance called *Spin Cycle* at the Brooklyn Museum. Participants were asked to pedal a stationary bicycle, which caused Robyn's spinning wheel to turn as she spun yarn from wool roving. Before mounting the bike, the cyclist was given a story-prompt card with text such as, "Tell me about your grandmother," or "What was your favorite piece of clothing as a child?" A mirror was placed on the floor so that the cyclist could look into Robyn's face while she spun, and she could see their face in return. The cyclist was encouraged to tell Robyn a story sparked from the prompt as they literally spun a "yarn," physical and verbal, in tandem.

Of the experience, Robyn said, "We looked in the mirror at each other and told stories while we worked together. The experience of hearing them and telling them was so beautiful, and working in collaboration to make yarn felt like a real connection. It was beyond all my expectations."

Over a period of several months in 2009, Robyn rode the #7 subway train from Queens into Manhattan for a performance

Video stills of Robyn Love's *Spindle 7*, 2009. Photos: Marcia Connolly, videographer

Video stills of Robyn Love's *Spindle 7*, 2009. Photos: Marcia Connolly, videographer

project called *Spindle 7*. As a passenger, Robin would sit and spin wool from a drop spindle, engaging in conversation with curious strangers. If they were interested in learning how to spin themselves, she gave them a lesson and provided them with a bag of wool and a spindle to take home with them. The project was based on Robyn's belief that spinning yarn is an activity found in almost every culture and that creating something would provide common ground between all the passengers who rode the subway together. The #7 line, the route that Robyn took from her home in Queens into Manhattan, serves the most ethnically diverse county in the United States, one with a large new immigrant population, thereby making it the perfect "incubator of what's happening in American culture right now."

"A lot of my art uses knitting, crochet, and other handwork," said Robyn. "I look to handwork as an excuse to reach people and engage with communities where it otherwise would be difficult."

As the project culminated, Robyn invited others to join her in spinning on the train. Having taught many of her fellow travelers to spin, Robyn said, "I see in people a kind of longing for something to make with their hands. When people are given this opportunity, they are ready for it. It is fulfilling in a way that so much of what else we do is not. On the train, and especially in New York City, you have your guard up a lot. Once you are willing to let your guard down, people are so amazing and generous, and they have fascinating stories."

Acknowledgments

I'd like to express my sincere gratitude to all who lent their support to me during the course of this project. I'd like to acknowledge the British Columbia Arts Council for their financial support, which not only provided funds to conduct research on the other side of the country, but more importantly, their grant gave me the emotional boost that I needed to take this project from the conceptual stage to reality.

Thank you to the volunteers and staff of the H.N. Pullar Library at the Textile Museum of Canada for your assistance with my research. We are lucky to have such a wonderful textile library and museum in this country. And thank you to Jessie Paterson and Vince Gladu for putting me up in Toronto and letting me write in your kitchen during the early weeks of Ash's life.

I'm thrilled that I was able to work with the talented photographer Jeanie Ow on this project. Thank you, Jeanie, for bringing your creativity and passion to each photograph. My gratitude goes out to the very photogenic Lucy Ly, Emily Smith, Rebecca Slaven, Steven Weigh, Usha Wennerstrand, and Storm Wennerstrand-Padmos who so patiently posed for photographs, and Gerilee McBride for her careful art direction. And, a sincere thank you to Anne Banner of Salmagundi West, Andrea and Rob Tucker of Got Craft, and Revolver Coffee for opening your doors to us.

The opportunity to bring this to Arsenal Pulp Press meant that I was able to work with a wonderful company of people once again. Thank you Brian Lam, Robert Ballantyne, Cynara Geissler, Susan Safyan, and Gerilee McBride. I feel privileged that I get to make my dream projects with such amazing people. Thank you for all of your hard work and support.

A shout out to scribblers Susannah Smith, Laura Farina, Erin Ashenhurst, Kim Clarke, Diane Farnsworth, and crafty gals Janet Brisson, Tanya Utenda, Mary Alice Elcock, and Kat Siddle. It is with your encouragement that this small seed of an idea came to germinate.

A special acknowledgment to Julia Monks for her careful and fast transcription work with artist interviews and to

Jaya Purswani for the technical editing and grading of the Close to the Heart sweater. And lastly, thanks to Paul Landry for providing feedback during the final editing stage on my manuscript.

A book such as this would not exist without participation of the artists, designers, writers, and photographers who choose to trust me with their work. A huge thank you to: Liz Aldag, Margaret Bennett, brifrischu, Leigh Bowser, Amanda Browder, Teresa Burrows, Diane Bush, Melissa A. Calderòn, Marion Coleman, Jennifer Cooper, Sarah Corbett, Maria Damon, Elizabeth Dancoes, Gina Dawson, Andrea Dezsö, Stephanie Dosen, Laura Farina, Chris Felver, Alixa Garcia, Eleanor Hannan, Paddy Hartley, Susan Kendal, Kerry Larkin, Sayraphim Lothian, Robyn Love, Hayley Madden, Bettina Matzkuhn, Anne Montgomery, Mark Newport, Iviva Olenick, Noël Palomo-Lovinski, Jennifer Annaïs Pighin, Naima Penniman, Sarah Quinton, Lea Redmond, Freddie Robins, Emily Smith, Philip Stearns, Tamar Stone, the UK Poetry Society, Sarah Terry, Jessica Vellenga, Kirsty Whitlock, Tracy Widdess, Howie Woo, Amanda Wood, Sherri Lynn Wood, Agustina Woodgate, Rosalind Wyatt, Carlyn Yandle, and Lindsay Zier-Vogel.

Index

Note: Page numbers in *italics* refer to images.

About the Author

Leanne Prain is the author of two other books for Arsenal Pulp Press: *Yarn Bombing: The Art of Crochet and Knit Graffiti* (with Mandy Moore) and *Hoopla: The Art of Unexpected Embroidery*. She has been writing about crafts, handmade communities, and design in various incarnations since 2005, and kept the infamous knit-graffiti blog *yarnbombing.com* from 2008 to 2012. Leanne holds a BFA in Creative Writing and Art History from the University of British Columbia and a Master in Publishing degree from Simon Fraser University. In her spare time, Leanne enjoys strong coffee, documentaries, hand-painted signage, silk-screening, walking around cities, and art galleries. Born in the Comox Valley on Vancouver Island, she lives and writes in Vancouver, British Columbia. *leanneprain.com*

About the Photographer

Jeanie Ow is a photographer who has documented weddings in North America, Asia, and Europe. Her highly sought-after photographic style stems from her love for the lost and found as well as a passion for storytelling the relationship of love between couples. Jeanie's work has been featured in publications such as *Wedluxe* and *Wedding Bells* magazines and includes editorial work in *Aislewalk* and *Heirloom Magazine*. When not composing through a viewfinder, Jeanie spends time with her dogs or learning how to knit and crochet. *jeanie.stu-di-o.com*